Testimonials for

"*Seven Seconds or Less* is written in a clear, easy-to-understand style that gives the business owner practical tools for reaching sound decisions on the present and future success of their business. Helen's focus on intuition becomes another valuable tool for individuals and business owners to help them assess situations and make informed decisions. Helen gave my company, Fitness and Wellness Insurance, an added advantage in the marketplace as she worked intuitively with us to design plans of action for better alignment of our management staff, and then guided us through the probabilities of potential candidates to purchase our company."

Jeffrey Frick, author of The Seventh Mindset,
and former CEO of Fitness and Wellness Insurance

"We brought Helen into our organization to make recommendations based on her intuition, and one year later her recommendations have proven to be right on the money! Many western people have lost their ability to make intuitive decisions. Helen has managed to retain this ability."

David Tett, President, Bushtracks Expeditions, Healdsburg CA

In ways both profound and practical, this book shows you proven ways to use your intuition in business. Grounded in evidence from business success stories, it helps you with strategies to access and develop confidence in your intuitive abilities. Engaging, inspiring and with lots of practical techniques, Helen Stewart guides you, step-by step, through the process of activating the power of intuition for your business and career. This is the kind of book we have been looking for in business!

Sally Rundle, PhD, international business coach
and intuitive consultant, Australia.

"I have known and consulted with Helen on both personal and professional matters for the past twelve years. Helen's advice and commentary have always been "bang on" and I don't make any major decisions without consulting with her! Helen's book, *Seven Seconds or Less: From Gut Feeling to Bottom Line* is a fabulous book—easy to read, entertaining and packed with Helen's wisdom. I will be recommending it to my colleagues and friends.

Jane Taras CPA/CA

"Attending Helen's workshops I learned to trust my good, strong gut feeling, listen to it, and act accordingly. It makes life much easier—and much more fun."

Benita Cantieni, Zurich, Switzerland

Seven Seconds or Less pulls you in with a variety of wonderful stories that illustrate Dr. Stewart's unique and compelling work in business intuition. I have read a lot of business books and none come close to delving into how to utilize our intuition (our "gut feelings") the way this book does. Dr. Stewart provides practical steps for honing your intuition and it has helped me understand the special gift she has so finely tuned.

Arden T. Reece, Marketing & Color Consultant,
Founder & Former CEO of Wardrobe 911

Today's competitive business climate is almost asymmetrical: what worked yesterday doesn't apply today. The need to be ahead of the innovation curve isn't always a product of the usual research efforts. Let this book assist you to find and use you and your team's intuitive strengths.

Bill Gregoricus, Consultant, Santa Fe, NM

Helen is an amazing individual with exceptional business acumen. Her professional and personal consulting is priceless.

Michelle Renee, San Francisco, CA

SEVEN SECONDS OR LESS

FROM GUT FEELING TO BOTTOM LINE IN CHALLENGING AREAS OF BUSINESS

Helen L. Stewart, Ph.D.

BALBOA.
PRESS
A DIVISION OF HAY HOUSE

Balboa Press books may be ordered through booksellers or by contacting:

Balboa Press
A Division of Hay House
1663 Liberty Drive
Bloomington, IN 47403
www.balboapress.com
1-(877) 407-4847

Because of the dynamic nature of the Internet, any web addresses or links contained in
this book may have changed since publication and may no longer be valid. The views
expressed in this work are solely those of the author and do not necessarily reflect the
views of the publisher, and the publisher hereby disclaims any responsibility for them.

The author of this book does not dispense medical advice or prescribe the use of any
technique as a form of treatment for physical, emotional, or medical problems without the
advice of a physician, either directly or indirectly. The intent of the author is only to offer
information of a general nature to help you in your quest for emotional and spiritual well-
being. In the event you use any of the information in this book for yourself, which is your
constitutional right, the author and the publisher assume no responsibility for your actions.

Any people depicted in stock imagery provided by Thinkstock are models,
and such images are being used for illustrative purposes only.
Certain stock imagery © Thinkstock.

Printed in the United States of America.

ISBN: 978-1-4525-7996-2 (sc)
ISBN: 978-1-4525-7998-6 (hc)
ISBN: 978-1-4525-7997-9 (e)

Library of Congress Control Number: 2013914846

Balboa Press rev. date: 10/03/2013

Dedication

To SP, HA, SC, and LM.
And to the unnamed clients, students, colleagues, and UMS
supporters who made the content of this book possible.

Preface

I t was common practice in the 1940s and '50s to perform tonsillectomies on children. Doctors believed the procedure would reduce the chance of catching polio, a communicable disease that was rampant at the time. We were living in Japan when my tonsils were removed; the year was 1953 and I was about ten years old.

My mother told me that while I was in the recovery room following the operation, I could speak only French. I had never studied French or traveled to a French speaking country. Once the anesthesia wore off, however, I returned to my normal English with no memory of the event. In many ways, that little incident was the beginning of a most extraordinary journey for me, of a life filled with questions that I continue to explore to this day.

How was that possible? Was this simply a physiological event? Why French and not some other language? Why contemporary French instead of archaic? Why did I forget the language afterwards? Was my experience speaking French in Japan a foreshadowing of future probabilities, or a harkening back to a time when French was my first language in some other time? *Where was this knowledge stored?*

From elementary school on, I began to read everything I could get my hands on about that particular phenomenon, and many other still unexplained synchronicities that fill my daily life. It is a short step indeed to go from unexplained French speaking to wondering about the nature of time and experiential probabilities. (I still know absolutely nothing about the mathematical ones!)

Incidentally, four years after my incident with the tonsils, my dad was stationed in France. Eventually I learned French fluently—in the usual ways—and continue to work in it today.

I have good paper, mind you: two high schools in France and several universities: Drew University, Boston University, Brandeis University, and Harvard University. I have also worked successfully in credible mainstream careers: university teacher and administrator, mediator and arbitrator, United Nations Development Program sociologist, simultaneous interpreter in French, and traditional business consultant. I am not entirely "out there." These careers spanned several decades, and yet all the while I have maintained a deep interest in things metaphysical: how do we know things with such a feeling of certainty, without knowing precisely *how* we know?

Fast forward to the 1990s. I was sitting with a colleague at lunch when she casually wondered how long it would take for her house to sell. "Three weeks," I blurted out. When the house sold in three weeks she told me about it with a rather strange look on her face that I still remember.

Some time later we were dealing with a temporary downturn in student enrollment based on current demographic data for high school seniors. We knew there would be a negative fiscal impact, but nobody knew exactly what the deficit would be. "Two and a half million dollars," I replied without hesitation.

For what seemed like endless months, multiple offices churned out numbers and scenarios trying to figure out what the deficit would be. By the time the answer finally came, I had left the university. Over a year later I received a telephone call from a former colleague: "Guess what the number was, Helen? Two and a half million." You had it exactly right! We laughed and that was that.

I knew then as I know now, that *something* is going on that permits us to know these things quickly and precisely. The challenge is figuring out *how* this happens, and then putting that ability to good use.

This book is my attempt to answer some of what began with my own questions about how to understand and apply what seems to me to be a universal ability. There are many other applications of intuition on demand in addition to the ones mentioned in this book; this is truly just a beginning.

Part One deals with the nature of intuition and what it takes to put it to good business use. It explains why focus, discernment, detachment from the outcome, and integrity are key for anyone intending to bring intuitive information into the workplace. It also takes a brief look at challenges presented by the use of intuitive data.

Part Two addresses three challenging areas in business that could benefit from a little intuitive help: mergers and partnerships, human resource management, and new product development. It also provides tools for looking intuitively at future probabilities to aid in strategic planning.

There are tips and tricks scattered throughout the book that you can use to develop your own intuitive abilities, or to tackle serious issues in a playful way with colleagues and friends.

Helen L. Stewart, Honolulu HI 16 May 2013

Table of Contents

List of Definitions, Tips, and Techniques

PART ONE

What is Seven Second Decision Making and How Does It Work?

How It All Began

atthew was a dot-com boomer and one of my first business clients. Young, savvy, well connected, supported by his family, and just plain gutsy, he gathered terrific people around him and dug in. Starting in the proverbial garage—in his case a right coast Brooklyn apartment—he used his computer programming skills to build a website for celebrity promotion and other hard-to-get content. Beginning in 1992, we worked and learned together intensively for several years and remain friends to this day. For a time he made money in a field that still had no clear revenue model, all the while garnering visibility for his creative genius. His little company went from zero to an estimated value of fifteen million dollars in one year. What dizzying excitement, seemingly endless possibilities; what FUN!

While he learned about online business, I learned about business intuition on demand. There are many stories to tell about those times in the Manhattan loft, including the emerging issue of intellectual property in digital environments. Some of those early questions continue to intrigue and plague, depending on your point of view. But for me, assessing potential strategic partnerships and preparing for surprise stand out above the rest. Regardless of size or domain, these are issues faced by organizations every day, loaded with land mines and with potentialities for success.

A larger company was interested in partnering with Matthew's company. These discussions involved meetings, proposals, counterproposals, estimations of valuation in an emerging market, intellectual property rights, and ultimately selling a product when there was as yet no proven revenue model for the Internet, then called the World Wide Web. "Who'll be there?" became a favorite game of ours during the negotiation process. "Who or what is the larger company, and who will be there to represent them? Whom do you need to bring with you to the next meeting to match their interest and agenda and personalities?" Using a few low-tech tools like making lists, framing questions, and finding a buddy who was willing to suspend disbelief for a moment and play these intuitive games, it was amazing to see the real-world impact of what can be learned in seven seconds or less. While I am typically not present for such negotiations, Matthew invited me to attend the signing ceremony once negotiations concluded. What a hoot to discover how closely the blind intuitive assessment matched the individuals once we met face-to-face!

Several interesting factors emerged. For example, there was intuitive evidence that a key player at the negotiating table would soon be leaving the larger organization, and as a result was less invested in the process than one might have imagined or expected if he were fully "in." He was in a hurry. This simple, unresearchable fact that the chief negotiating attorney was on his way out proved to be an important tidbit for Matthew's company, resulting in a tactical shift and successful conclusion to the negotiation. There were many other factors as well, naturally. The point here is the importance of surprise that comes with the regular, intentional use of intuitive tools in the business world.

A second key element emerged in Matthew's story, also based on surprise, I received clear intuitive indications that Leo, Matthew's co-founder and vice-president, was planning to leave their own company very soon as well; not just the attorney from the potential partner company. When I passed the information on to Matthew and suggested strongly he plan for Leo's departure, he dismissed the leaving as impossible since the two had built the company together. He just could not imagine making the business work without his sidekick and business partner.

Two months later Leo, the vice president of Matthew's company, was gone under rather unseemly circumstances. Matthew's heart was broken, but he was prepared in advance, even if still unbelieving. I could not save him from the heartbreak, but I could help him save the company by preparing for a succession plan in the event Leo did leave.

In addition to the lesson for Matthew, there was another important lesson for me as a professional business intuitive: just because the information you receive is unwelcomed at the time, it doesn't mean you are wrong. When you feel strongly about your gut feeling, stick to your guns and go with it!

That set of experiences was the start of a wild ride on my path to the mastery of business intuition on demand, or what I like to call Seven Second Decision Making. Since the time with Matthew, I have worked with publicly traded companies and sole proprietorship entrepreneurs, non-profit organizations, politicians, artists, spiritual practitioners, software developers, the hospitality industry, and a host of individuals trying to figure out their purpose in life.

There will be much more to say about strategic partnerships and other challenges facing contemporary businesses, but first let's tackle the basics: what is intuition, and what in the world can complex businesses start to figure out in seven seconds or less?

Blink

In 2005, Malcolm Gladwell's best selling book *Blink: The Power of Thinking Without Thinking* hit the stands and revolutionized our understanding of lightning-speed decision making. The book flap says, "*Blink* reveals that great decision makers aren't those who process the most information or spend the most time deliberating, but those who have perfected the art of 'thin-slicing'—filtering the very few factors that matter from an overwhelming number of variables.[1]" His powerful chapter entitled "Seven Seconds in the Bronx," recounts how Guinean immigrant Amadou Diallo was killed by the New York police, based on errors of split-second observational data processed by policemen who saw him standing in front of his apartment building around midnight. When Diallo reached for his keys, the four officers thought he was reaching for a gun and shot him 41 times.

Gladwell makes the point that we can process enormous amounts of data in seven seconds, as the police did in evaluating what Amadou Diallo was doing on that step at midnight. First, he didn't look like he belonged there. Second, there was a lot of drug dealing in that neighborhood so the officers assumed malevolent intent. Their conclusions were based on nanosecond observational data gained through professional experience.

Fifteen years prior to the publication of *Blink*, I was teaching small groups of students in my living room how to develop their intuitive abilities, including how to come up with information in seven seconds or less. Most of our intuitive "targets" were not physically present, so Gladwell's observational "Blink," and Eckman and Friesen's five-hundred-page Facial Action Coding System (FACS),[2] were simply of no use to us. We were getting very specific information about people known to only one person in the room, people who were not present to give physical clues. Something else was going on, and some aspects of how intuition works still remain a mystery to me. We did not need a five hundred-page manual to "get" open-ended information about what was going on with a stranger in another part of the country or the world. How was that possible?

For decades I have worked with clients over the phone, online, and by email; I knew absolutely nothing except a name. I would eventually meet some who became regular clients, but in those years before Skype and other visual meeting software there were no visual clues, and often not even sound, as consults would be typed by me on the computer, often alone in the middle of the night.

We process inordinate amounts of very complex information very quickly. I have found that the best way to get to information that we know, without knowing how we know, is to *speed up* the process and to begin blathering what seems like made-up information before the rational mind can kick in. That is the reason for the *seven seconds or less* rule. As we become more sophisticated with the process, seven seconds will actually feel like an eternity.

In college I had a summer job in a factory just outside Boston that manufactured tennis shoes. We worked on conveyor belts, and the task on my night shift was to complete over a thousand pair of tennis shoes in eight hours. My individual job was to move the metal last that held the shoe-in-process from one conveyor belt to the other, and to put latex on the toe once the sole had been attached. Not too challenging for someone with dreams of someday earning a Ph.D.

The first week I thought I was going to die. There was no way I could keep up with the pace of the relentless movement of that conveyor belt. But after a couple of weeks I felt as if I could run around the building between shoes! Boredom became the biggest challenge, not meeting the goal to make a thousand pair of sneakers per night.

The same principle applies to intuition. Initially you might think it impossible to get meaningful information in seven *minutes*, let alone seven seconds. But as you become accustomed to just diving into what I like to think of as a unified field of knowledge, a mere *second* between the framing of a question and the intuitive response might begin to feel slow.

The more time you have to think, the less time you have to intuit. It is that simple.

Intuition is a Liberal Art

It is not magic: rather, like reading, writing, calculating, strategic planning, or critical thinking, it is simply another tool for success in the world of business.

So What is Seven Second Decision Making?

even Second Decision Making is the natural blend of reason, experience and intuition. In a remarkably brief moment the mind can sift through endless data and simply *know* the best course of action or most likely outcome for business or life. It is knowing repeatedly and with certainty, without understanding exactly how one knows. It is gut feeling on demand with high levels of accuracy, and it can have an extraordinary impact on business success and personal fulfillment, beginning in seven seconds or less.

It is a methodology, a process for obtaining consistent, accurate, ethical, insight-on-demand, for me especially in the domains of business and frontier science. All other domains, of course, enjoy equal access with equal ease. Intuition both uses surprise and forewarns of its occurrence.

Seven Second Decision Making requires:

- **Focus**: this and only this. In a field of many variables and almost limitless probabilities, what is the most likely course of events? What information is available to change the most probable course, if it is a desired one, and to arrive at the chosen destination or outcome with the greatest amount of ease?
- **Interpretation**: knowledge of context. What does the information mean for this person or this company or this

situation at this time? Are there symbols to be interpreted, or images, or numbers, or emotions? Interpretation is possible when the other tools are strong.

- **Discernment**: the capacity to distinguish. What is mine? What is yours? What is truly relevant in this particular situation?
- **Integrity**: only the highest ethical standards will do. No implicit or explicit conflicts of interest.
- **Trust**: in the self; in the other; in the future; in the world; in human nature; in fundamental good intention; in life itself.

Intuition is the Foundation for Seven Second Decision Making

Since this is principally a self-help book rather than an academic one, I focus minimally on the lively theoretical debate in business literature about the definition and reliability of intuition. There are many resources that define intuition principally as "pattern recognition," including articles in the *Harvard Business Review* and other mainstream refereed academic journals. At least they are talking about it! Cutting right to the chase, and for my purposes here, these are my assertions:

- Unprovable Assertion: Intuition makes it possible to pick up information about anything in the known and unknown universe in seven seconds or less.
- Demonstrable assertion: Using intuition, people can come up with useful and repeatedly accurate information about unknown people, places, things, and businesses.

For a time I was on the speaker's bureau of a national organization that supports the personal and professional development of CEOs. In one of those workshops I asked if any of the fairly skeptical participants were working on a new product that had not been shared outside the company. One man in particular raised his hand and agreed to play along with our little intuition game. I'll call him Robert. This happened near the beginning of the workshop, so no one in the room had received any training on business uses of intuition.

I asked the other members of the group to describe the product Robert's company was working on. "Just start babbling," I instructed them. By the way, each CEO support group is constructed in such a way as to avoid placing potential business competitors in the same group. In this way members could be as open as possible in their discussions with each other.

Right away people started throwing out descriptive phrases, feelings, words, and images. We eventually filled up several sheets of butcher-block paper with descriptions of this very secret new product: how long it would take to complete; what marketing or production challenges the company might face with the product; how the company would be doing two, five, and ten years from now; and what one piece of advice each member would give to Robert. One group member even jumped up spontaneously and drew a picture of what he thought the product looked like!

When we finished, our volunteer Robert was free to tell us only what he felt comfortable divulging in feedback to the group members. By the time this exercise was over, not only he, but also everyone else in the room was picking his or her jaw up off the floor. This collaborative effort, this very short game, resulted in an uncanny description of the new secret product under development in Robert's company, and he ended up sharing enough to prove the point: *everybody is intuitive and anybody can tap into that capacity at any time on demand.*

There are many additional questions that could be raised about this instance of intuition at work, including questions of privacy and business ethics. There were controls in place so that Robert could not give clues through body language. But for now let's just say that it is possible for people to get information about other people and companies in seven seconds or less with no formal training. That is my assertion. Whether this latent talent is acknowledged or developed is quite another matter, but the capacity is there.

- **Intuition is a continuous signal that provides information about the nature of the whole or any of its component parts**. For me, the whole is literally *All That Is*, and that includes all that could ever be. I believe this signal to be comprised of energy "signatures" that operate in both material and non-material domains.

- **Intuition can reach beyond past and present to identify, interpret, and actually *create* patterns in the future**, as easily as it *responds* to those future patterns in the here and now, or *recognizes* them from the past.

- ***Intuition is not bound by linear equations.*** The mind can bounce from one type of information or processing to another without skipping a beat, and can link the rational, emotional, data driven, observational, and intuitive together as pearls in a single strand of necklace. Working in a domain outside space and time, intuition permits non-sequiturs and apparent nonsense to flow into the conscious mind without having to be linked rationally to any past pattern or action. In this unusual way, pivotal factors that might otherwise be eliminated from consideration can be considered together, forming new and as yet unrecognizable patterns for the future.

- In my view intuition is the non-verbal language of the cosmos. *I call intuition language because its purpose is communication—* within, between, and among parts of the whole—whatever the parts look like, act like, or become. It is intuition that holds the whole together, moving in unison like a flock of birds flying south for the winter, dipping, diving, turning in mind-boggling synchrony, heading sometimes for a destination they have never seen, but know exists. Each particle has its own signature and is aware of its own existence and the existence of all other units of the whole. It does not matter whether these units are identified individually or collectively as they change form and expression; their identity is inviolate and known by all others. That is my worldview, and that is how I believe I can do what I do effectively. In his book *Entangled Minds,*[3] especially the chapters on "Gut Feelings" and "Theories of PSI," Dean Radin does a superb of explaining better than I ever could how it is I know what I know.

Characteristics of Intuition

○ **More than an educated guess . . . it is deep knowing**
○ **Gut feeling: literally grabs you in your belly**
○ **Feeling that you have encountered absolute truth**
○ **Uncanny feeling of familiarity or precognition**
○ **Certainty without knowing how or why you are certain**
○ **Shiver, throbbing, or tingling in the body offering different meanings at different times**
○ **Pattern recognition, based primarily on past visual, social, and mathematical models**
○ **"Divine guidance" for the religious, or what scientists might call "inspiration"**
○ **Connection with everyone and everything else**
○ **Something that holds together what some scientific and metaphysical cosmologists call a self-aware, dynamic, interactive, unified field of consciousness**
○ **It has something to do with probabilities and time**

Business applications of intuition take special advantage of this "connection to the whole" to provide an intuitive edge for human resource decisions, new product development, and global financial markets. The developed hunch can flesh out the impact or consequences of decisions made now, thereby avoiding financial or productivity pitfalls in the future.

Because we are connected to the whole through our capacity for intuition, we can compute probabilities in a flash and identify the most probable outcome of any particular action or choice from any moment in time. What a boon to business!

> "Intuition does not denote something contrary to reason, but something outside of the province of reason."—Carl Jung

- **Intuition is not a substitute for scientific inquiry and quantitative data; it is a different and additional tool** using the inner senses rather than the outer ones.
- **Intuition can provide foresight and insight into possible scientific discoveries before the technology and research have been developed to "prove" their validity.** By their own admission, thoughtful scientists routinely use intuition; including scientists who have been widely acclaimed for certain mainstream discoveries. Einstein helped a bit with his famous quotes on imagination and intuition, but it is still tricky to be "out" as an intuitive in the natural sciences for fear of being ridiculed. The time is fast approaching, though, when intuition can be an open partner to business and science, rather than its mistress.

Seven Second Decision Making involves the conscious use of intuition in everyday life. It holds the promise of transforming the nature of personal, social, political, and business relationships. It also helps us pay attention to what we know without knowing how we know, and, as we learn to trust that deep knowing, makes it easier to collaborate productively. Intuition also makes it harder to be fooled or manipulated.

> "Even executives who believe passionately in the value of rigor concede that there are limits to objective analysis. After all, facts don't speak for themselves; one has to make sense of the facts, not just get them straight."—Sutcliffe and Weber[3]

Interpreting Intuitive Information

Getting an intuitive hunch or "hit" is one thing; knowing precisely what it means and what to do with it is quite another. What does the information mean? To whom should I mention the idea? How do I know how to make sense out of what comes in the form of gut feeling? For example, "I dreamed of an elephant running from a mouse . . . does this have something to do with the stock market or our new product launch?"

Interpreting intuitive information, particularly in ways that make sense and support business decision making, is an art as well as a skill that can be learned. The old "garbage in—garbage out" model of information applies to intuitive information as well as any other source.

> Data—literary or economic—have no inherent meaning. They acquire meaning by our bringing meaning to them. And different people, with different experiences, will construct different meanings.[4]

Through my own experience with business applications of intuition, I am convinced that unique life experience enhances the intuitive process rather than hinders it. Idiosyncratic experience develops a personal lexicon for accurate and reliable interpretations of intuitive data.

First of all, the information comes in a form that most quickly and easily matches the history and experience of the person receiving it.

You do not have to be a Joseph Campbell, Carl Jung, or Sigmund Freud to make sense out of intuitive information. The principal challenge initially is to interpret the information within a framework that makes sense to *you*. Only after that does the challenge arise of having the information make sense to somebody else. So interpretation occurs on at least two levels: the one who receives the direct information as a consultant or employee of the organization; and the decision maker with authority to act on the interpretation of raw data received through intuited sources or processes. Each party in the process has its own system of relevances[4], beliefs, and cues. Bridging the gap between one set of perceptions and another is challenging, and it is at this juncture that most errors of interpretation and meaning occur.

Henry VIII may have great meaning to me and absolutely none to the person to whom I wish to communicate the essence of this intuitive clue. The other person may have no context for such an historical figure, and perhaps never heard of this English king. In order for the accurate information to have meaning to the second party, I have to place it in a context relevant to the decision maker.

Interestingly enough, intuition provides both the initial meaning and the tools to *translate* the meaning for the other party to the process. I have learned that the "blathering process" actually comes up with specific words that make sense to the client, even when the words make no sense to me. I remember, for example, speaking with a software developer about a consistent metaphor having to do with a cart and horse. I felt that something needed to be before rather than after, reversing what he was currently designing. I knew nothing about software at the time, so the metaphor meant little to me. He just laughed and told me he was wondering whether he needed to develop a front-end component to the software product under development, rather than to place that component as a back-end application. What I told him made perfect sense to him.

Receiving and interpreting intuitive information on demand can be taught with a few relatively simple techniques, but it might take a lifetime to perfect, just like learning the one-hundred-eight tai chi moves. With daily practice the content becomes more and more fluid, more accurate and reliable, more predictive for future action, and more developed for complex decision making.

It is commonly said that the arbiter of a dream's meaning is ultimately the dreamer himself. It is no different with intuitive interpretation. When offered intuitive business information, the CEO or senior manager will know if the information makes sense, and if the interpretation of the information is on the mark. Sometimes this assessment of value cannot be fully comprehended until future events bear out those interpretations and predictions. Sometimes the recipient of the information will resist the content and not want to hear "bad news" or an undesired outcome, thereby discounting accurate and timely information. This is not an exact science; on the other hand, neither is it an exact science when someone offers the manager charts, graphs, and the promise to solve complex and perhaps insoluble structural problems through numerical algorithms alone.

Each industry, company, group, and individual has shared and unique interpretations of information. It is only through repetition and good record keeping that interpretations become reliable. These records are kept in the mind and body of its leaders and employees, as well as on paper or in electronic files. Intuitive records are actually a different form of institutional memory! I have learned in private practice that any and every aspect of individual life experience contributes to the symbolism of intuitive information and to the ability to process information quickly and accurately.

Quite literally, any element or idea in the remotest corner of the conscious and subconscious mind can be used to help produce and sort out intuitive data. This element or idea is the source of flexibility, unpredictability, change, and also of enormous success or potential failure.[5]

Cultural groups may share some symbols. I may think of betrayal, for example, and notice that there is a throbbing or tingling sensation in the middle of my back. Or I may see a mental picture of someone being stabbed in the back. If the question has to do with a potential partnership, then I might interpret the information as a signal that the potential partner may not have the client's best interest in mind. This information alone is not enough to decide partnership decisions, but may trigger further probing and analysis using other methods in conjunction with additional intuitive probing.

Other intuitive symbols may spring from uniquely individual experience; sometimes they are embedded within culturally relevant images and sometimes they are completely idiosyncratic in origin. For example, when I receive intuitive information concerning unbridled drive on the part of an individual or company, the image that comes to mind is a photograph of Henry VIII that I recall seeing in my junior high school textbook. Others in military schools or various regions of the country may have used the same text, but the image may not have stuck with them the way it did with me. Henry VIII's face was hidden, but his hat and ermine cape were visible from the perspective of one looking at his back and a profile of his face. That image eventually reappeared decades later as an intuitive personal clue that the issue of ambition at all costs was relevant to an individual or company. Eventually, the full color copy of my mental image of a famous oil painting of Henry VIII turned into a two-line pen and ink scribble on a blank piece of paper. The symbol represents for me situations in which one party would stop at nothing to get its way, in much the same way as Henry VIII ridded himself of his various wives and established the Church of England in order to impose his will on the country. The image has become part of my personal lexicon, added to many others over the years. It is a kind of shorthand that helps me understand complex interpersonal or interparty relationships quickly, consistently, and accurately. The image itself is not especially complex, nor can it singlehandedly help one select among complex options for future action. Furthermore, the symbol represents no emotional judgment; it is simply a pointer to some of the dynamics which must be understood and investigated further in the decision making process. For example, it can help determine whether a potential partnership might be pursued or should be avoided.

The Henry VIII metaphor is neither linear thinking nor irrational fantasy. It is much more complex, happening in a nanosecond. Intuition provides the leading edge that all innovators and entrepreneurs seek to understand so they can influence their particular market, especially when blended with other analytical and decision making tools.

Interpretations become accepted over time, as clues associated with those interpretations are consistently accurate and predictive for the business. Symbolic interpretations become shorthand responses to simple yes/no questions, and to much more complex organizational issues as well in concentrated form. In my own experience shorthand clues and interpretations seem to "stick," especially when they are experienced visually or physiologically. Once an intuitive clue is mapped to a mental or physiological response, the clue repeats without prompting in very reliable ways time and time again. The triggering of these clues is still a mysterious process to me, but the clues themselves are always relevant to the situation at hand.

Another clue for me personally is a tingling sensation at the top of the head. This means the individual or company is dealing with logistical issues, problems of daily life. Why that sensation in that location of my body? I don't know, but the feeling and meaning are connected and consistent. The tingling returns in a nanosecond and I am off and running with more information that is attuned to the issues of the *particular* individual or challenging logistical situation.

The Statue of Liberty before the World Trade Center Collapse. A similar photo appeared afterwards from the same vantage point, but this time the Towers were gone and the Statue of Liberty stood on her own.

"She Goes On Her Own:" Interpreting Metaphors

It is important to discern whether intuitive hunches should be interpreted quite literally, or whether they should be taken as a clue related to something else that is not literal at all. Stories abound of dreams and other types of premonitions about the World Trade Center collapse on September 11, 2001, a stock market crash, earthquakes, and other significant mass events. Only through hindsight, however, does interpretation become crystal clear.

For example, here is an intuitive insight I published on an old website in 2001, exactly as posted at the time, one month before the attack on the World Trade Center:

> *August 13, 2001*
> *Image: The phrase 'She goes on her own'" The 'she' is a well-known individual or political leader, or the Statue of Liberty.*

Meanings:

1. *There is the possibility of an announcement by Hillary Clinton that she will formally divorce her husband.*
2. *The country separates and isolates itself further from ideals of liberty and privacy. The Statue of Liberty goes on her own, no longer connected to the historical legacy of her people. Some new legislation is written or passed that limits personal freedom, or some action is taken to limit prior collaboration between the USA and its European colleagues.*

While unsurprising, there is sadness on both counts. When liberty must set herself apart and go on her own in order to be free, the world weeps for her and for itself. It weeps for lost innocence, lost hope, lost legacy."

The column included a statement that the Statue of Liberty "goes on her own." At the time it was uncertain whether that intuitive hunch had something to do with Hillary Clinton, who may have been in the news at that time, the United States, or the city of New York. Clinton did not announce a divorce. Following the World Trade Center disaster, however, numerous national magazines published photographs of the Statue of Liberty no longer flanked by the World Trade Center towers in the background: "She [the Statue] goes on her own."

The article also included references to the world's weeping for lost freedom. As a result of the attacks on September 11th, the President and legislators abolished a century's worth of hard won domestic freedoms overnight as the United States moved into military readiness through passage of The Patriot Act and a raft of Executive Orders.

This is a perfect example of the combination of intuitive information in metaphorical form that also hinted at literal events. It takes skill, practice, and the benefit of hindsight to know for certain what interpretation to give to intuitive information like that.

If someone had asked me the meaning of my very own column in August 2001, it is unlikely I could have said with clarity that there would be a mass event on the order of September 11, 2001. Had I gotten close enough to assume a mass event of great importance, I might have more likely interpreted the information to have direct bearing on the Statue of Liberty, not on the World Trade Towers. The photographs were stark evidence of something regarding the Statue of Liberty's going on her own, but the deeper meaning was much more extraordinary: the obliteration of the Towers, and also of the sense of confidence, peace, privacy, and safety in the world. The interpretation might also have signaled increased displeasure with the policies of the United States as the country's invasion of Iraq went against domestic and international public opinion. Had someone asked additional follow-up questions, which often occurs in regular "salons" I hold or sessions for clients, then we might have fleshed out more detail regarding interpretation and literal meaning of these now extraordinary words.

Imagine that the information you receive is a metaphor, rather than something literal: would that change anything for you? Sometimes intuitive information is actually *meant* to be more metaphorical than literal. For example, images of an airplane crash could be quite literal for a business traveler, prompting him or her to postpone or cancel a flight. On the other hand, the image of a crash could be an indication that the present course of action or investment will trigger unforeseen consequences of a negative nature for the individual, company, a particular stock or commodity, or the market in general.

Only time, practice, attention, and increasingly honed ability can make full use of intuitive information about business opportunities or challenges. With regular practice, however, the interpretation of complex situations becomes more and more specific and refined. Hitting target numbers occurs more quickly, with smaller deviations from the actual, as the data are measured and corroborated over time.

Basic Tips for Seven Second Decision Making

○ Trust your gut feelings, even if they don't make rational sense; then find out later how you know what you know

○ Trust the gut feelings of others and encourage their expression in the workplace

○ *Do not edit*, no matter how tempting it feels to do so

○ When you frame intuitive questions, *avoid leading questions* and ask for an open-ended *best* option, whether or not you have already considered a specific set of rational choices

○ Accept and trust the *very first image* or idea you receive; sort out the "why" later

○ *Describe* images or phrases in detail before interpreting them

○ Remember to *ask* if there are additional issues or parties to consider

○ Accuracy requires detachment from the outcome: *learn* simple techniques for discernment and detachment

○ *Practice*

○ As we say here in Hawaii, *talk story*. Communicate non-linear information to each other."

That's the Workshop!

What I taught Robert's group when they figured out his secret project could be summarized on a 5x8 card, just like the one above. Dive in and trust that the gobbledygook that seems to come up from out of nowhere actually has meaning. If the meaning seems not for you, then perhaps there is meaning for the person or project you are thinking about. That is the fun and the power of intuition!

What is critical, and this takes practice, is that you speak the *very first thought* that pops into your mind. It is amazing how quickly we can go through five or six thoughts in just a few seconds, followed by a natural and rational desire to edit. Take the *first* response, even if that first one doesn't make any sense. That is the element of surprise that will make your heart sing later.

The rational mind is highly trained, and it will jump in to sort things out in expected ways in a nanosecond if you permit it, based on what you already know and expect. For example, when I told my trader client the price of oil in a year, his rational mind was quick to compute the current price of oil and to determine that my answer lay outside the realm of possibility. Don't let your reason save you this time, if only for a quick moment. Just go with the nonsense and follow the first thought to see where it leads. Sometimes you can have five thoughts in a single second. Wend your way back mentally to the very *first* thought and follow that one. Discernment here is important.

One key indicator for me that I have entered the realm of intuitive information happens when I find myself saying, "But that just doesn't make any sense." Or, "I don't know what this means, but I am getting a strong sense that this person will not go the whole way with you to completion of the project." That person may be the best candidate on paper, but there may be other factors at play that the paper does not and cannot show. For example, the individual may be untrustworthy and immediately go after your job, or the job of the person to whom he or she will report directly; or the person may end up leaving in six months, right after you have invested all of that training time with little or no return.

Surprise is the single most important element in realizing that you have stumbled into the realm of the intuitive. Often what doesn't make any rational sense makes a whole lot of sense in the larger scheme of things. But you won't be able to know what sense it makes until later. In the meantime you have to trust yourself, go with the first thought, detach from the outcome, and just wait to see what develops. That's the tough part: the waiting for confirmation that you were or were not on target. When there are lots of dollars and huge reputations at stake, the waiting can seem like an eternity.

That is why TRUST is at the top of the list of tips: trust in yourself, and trust in the fundamental good intention of others. If anything can derail accurate intuitive information in a heartbeat, it is the lack of trust. Trust does not mean that you throw away your natural skepticism, or that you stop looking for corroboration through rational methods. Trust means that you are willing to suspend disbelief for a moment, just long enough to dart out into the universe and pick up something that might be useful in resolving the issue at hand, something that all too often might be ignored.

Detachment from the Outcome

O h my! Here is the wake-up call for all of us control freaks out there. If you are used to managing crises, to being in control, to being invested in the outcome, because investment in the outcome is the true mark of loyalty in a company, you have some homework to do now.

Detachment from the outcome does not mean you no longer care. It means that you are willing to let your ego and your fear step aside for a moment. If you are attached to the outcome, you will be closed to the element of surprise, and to information that comes to your aid from outside the domain of reason. It is very hard to remain detached when you know that millions and billions of dollars are riding on your decision. And yet that is precisely what you have to do when you work with intuitive information.

The toughest business clients for me have been small-scale investors and day traders. They have chosen intensity as their domain, watching feverishly as stocks and commodities move up and down endlessly throughout the trading day. Their emotions move at warp speed as well, following every tick up or down and every available chart. It is practically impossible to get them to slow down enough to listen to the advice they sought. And it is also harder for me to stay detached when the clients are in a dither. But if I don't keep my cool while others around me are losing theirs, I am useless to them, just as you are useless to your business if you are running around at a fever pitch all day every day, even on weekends.

There is little room for intuitive information to sneak past all those barricades, built on neither reason nor trust. For some individuals the marketplace is filled with piranhas and sharks, so they must keep on the move or be devoured. The love-hate relationship with money and markets has eroded fundamental trust in human nature, especially when small investors keep getting burned.

If you work in such a field it is critical that you stop first, take a deep breath, and center yourself before you attempt to receive intuitive information. You must be able to detach from the outcome for a split second and mean it; it must be long enough to know what action, *if any*, would be best for you to undertake.

Recognizing the challenges, some individuals and companies have developed rational protocols to ensure detachment from the outcome, especially if they use intuition professionally. For a brief time I worked with others on a remote viewing project designed by a colleague. Wikipedia defines remote viewing as "the practice of seeking impressions about a distant or unseen target through extra-sensory perception using subjective means, in particular, extra-sensory perception (ESP) or 'sensing with mind.'"[6] Although sets of envelopes with viewing "targets" were prepared in advance, the tests were double-blind, in that no one knew which envelopes would be selected for the weekly experiment. In fact, the object we were to view was not actually chosen—again blind protocol—until the week *after* our results were in. I will avoid saying too much about the exciting phenomenon Dean Radin calls "retrocausation"[7] for the time being. Suffice it to say that the viewers were just trying to identify objects in hidden envelopes. The designers of the test, however, had other plans. The information from our remote viewing experiments would provide them clues to the direction of financial markets!

It was hard enough to be detached while just trying to figure out what was in those envelopes. Had I known that there was money riding on our answers, it would have been harder still to remain detached enough to provide solid information. That is why the investigative team had to construct the process in such a way that no one with an emotional or financial investment could insert that emotion into the process—at least, not on the surface of things.

Trust is first, but detachment from the outcome has to be running a close second. You have to be able to let go of what others might think, and you have to let go of the possibility that your intuitive information might be wrong. Remember, quantitative analysis is often wrong as well. Trust your gut, and then act on what it tells you in as detached a manner as possible. Repeated practice with positive results is the best way to settle down and become more and more willing to detach from the outcome of any particular moment's issues.

Discernment: To Speak or Not to Speak; That is the Question

An important corollary to the issue of interpreting intuitive information is the sticky area of discernment. Not only must you interpret the information with repeated relevance and accuracy, it is equally as important to be certain that the information should indeed be communicated. If it is appropriate to communicate, then in what form, when, and to whom? Is this information for your own action or understanding only? Should this information be passed on to your team? Is this information relevant to the subject at hand, or should it sit on the back burner for future discussion at an appropriate time? All of these are questions of discernment, the answers to which can also be supplied through intuitive responses, as well as through other objective indicators in the work environment.

Discernment

- Would this be better left unsaid?
- What is the purpose of the information?
- Who is served by the information? You personally? The company?
- Should the information from my gut feeling be communicated directly or indirectly?
- How does my self-interest color or distort the information?
- Imagine that the information you receive is a metaphor, rather than something literal: would that change anything for you?

Even when the intuitive information received is right on the money, useful, and relevant, some things are better left unsaid. You can use that information to help with human resource management or organizational restructuring, but you may be wiser not to state the information directly. For example, you may be aware that what is offered to you as a presenting issue has a deeper issue at its core, which remains unnamed by any parties to the discussion. You may choose to respond publicly to the presenting issue only, deciding not to go deeper at this time, or you could address the deeper issue in some indirect way without "laying it all out on the table."

Knowing when to keep silent is an art. Some individuals feel that every thought passing through their minds must be shared, whether or not the audience is interested. When this type of individual approaches, people take cover to avoid the barrage. It is unnecessary to name everything you know, even if you are correct in your assessment of the situation with the aid of intuitive information. There is nothing to prove. Ask yourself the question, "Is this thought better left unsaid?" If the first answer is yes, then keep it to yourself and assume that the thought was for your own edification and assistance, but not necessarily for sharing with the world.

- **What is the purpose of the information?**

Is the intuitive information designed to lead you, to lead others, and/or to shape the company? Is the goal to make someone else wrong or right, or to further the work? Should you use the information metaphorically or literally or both? Discernment requires that you understand fully, without fooling yourself or anyone else as to the true purpose for its use. If you are contemplating layoffs, for example, it would not be appropriate to claim intuited information as a basis for ridding the company of a person or group or division that you have wanted to see gone for a long time. Intuition is a key resource for making tough decisions, but it is not to be used as your only tool, as a kind of "divine right" to lead by whim.

Ultimately, the goal of intuitive information is to *serve*. Period. During the time leading up to the financial crisis of 2008 I kept getting repeat messages for a financial services client that something big with negative consequences was going to happen; the company needed to hold cash. Those messages began bombarding my awareness twelve to eighteen months before the market crash that was triggered by the subprime mortgage situation. I wasn't looking for bad news, was clearly not a Wall Street insider, and had no access to privileged information. I just felt that a disaster was brewing, and wasn't even certain as to the nature of any potential problem. All I knew was that my client needed to hold cash.

I still remember one of our lunch meetings when he asked me, "Helen, do you still see a disaster looming?" I felt guilty that I didn't have better news for him, but I simply nodded my head and replied, "Yes." My goal was to serve that client with the best I had to offer. Many times I thought I was becoming a doomsayer, but by this time I had learned to trust the information I got and to pass it on without editing. As events began to unfold, once again intuition had come to the rescue. Now I knew that the persistent sense of foreboding was offering help to avoid disaster. Because of mutual trust, my client's company survived and eventually thrived following considerable struggle, while many others went under. Thousands of individuals and communities went under as well. If more of us took advantage of warnings about excess and disaster and paid attention to proddings about probabilities for success and thriving, we might stop risky behavior *before* jumping or falling over the cliff, and have better news to anticipate.

- **Who is served by the information: You personally?**
  The company? Both?

When you are an interested party, it is impossible to be fully detached from the outcome and content of intuitive information. It is critical to discern who is most served by both analytical and intuitive data. Just because you are presented with spreadsheets, it does not necessarily follow that the information is objective because you are looking at numbers. Likewise, just because you are presented with intuitive information, you need not assume that the information is only subjective because you are working with gut feelings. Those feelings could derive from an astute understanding of the data.

With one notable exception, I made a decision early on in this profession to be financially as divested and neutral as possible from any client or company with whom I worked. Maybe it's my old Methodist upbringing; I'd like to believe it has something to do with finally achieving some sense of integrity in my life. What I know for certain is that I just work better, and intuition just works better, when I am as detached from the outcome as possible.

Now if the client is paying me, I still have some vested interest in the success of that client and the success of the client's business; I cannot escape every element of attachment, no matter how hard I try.

The very best way to eliminate self-interest is to have intuitive information come from a third party source using double-blind techniques. Ask someone who knows nothing about the situation to choose off the top of the head from a list of options you wrote down in advance. But this is not always possible, and you still need to develop your own intuitive capacities. You can (and should!) frame the question for yourself, all the while remembering that you are an interested party, and then compare that information with what you hear from disinterested sources. I will provide more detail about this in Part II. Factoring in self-interest is critical, especially as questions and situations become more complex. It is easy to find self-interest lurking behind numbers and hidden within strategic plans and computer models.

It is possible, of course, that self-interest and the interest of the company converge, whether you are its CEO or a lower-level employee. Do not assume that self-interest is important or noticeable only at senior management levels where ultimate decision-making authority lies. Many studies show that every individual in a company must make on-the-spot decisions on a daily basis.[8] These decisions, whether or not motivated by altruistic impulses, have short—or long-term implications for both the individual and the company as a whole.

There is often rancor between management and labor, especially unionized labor right now. Truth be told, owner, manager, and employee would all be in deep trouble if the company failed. Furthermore, the customer has a special interest in the success of that business, or the individual would not be or remain a customer. That is why it is so important to find the good intention that always lurks beneath the surface of seemingly adversarial relationships.

- **Should the information from my gut feeling be communicated directly or indirectly?**

It is actually possible to use intuition itself to determine whether intuitive information should be communicated directly or indirectly. Just ask, and take the *very* first response you get. The process could be framing a simple yes-no question. You could also decide in your own mind that "1" means directly and "2" means indirectly. Then ask a colleague who is not involved in the issue to choose between 1 and 2 without telling the person anything about the meaning of those numbers. Use the response to structure how you communicate the information.

Most importantly, in a business setting information should be translated or translatable into standard business language before putting it out directly into the workplace. Even if you have fostered the development and use of intuition in your work setting, it would be inappropriate to begin a meeting with, "An hour ago I had a vision that Verithane might be interested in partnering with our company." However you could easily say something like "It occurred to me ..." or "I was wondering if..." or "What do you think about the possibility of approaching Verithane as our strategic partner?"

In the latter examples the information has made its way from the domain of intuition into an ordinary business context with a simple shift in language. As in any other area of human communication, *any* content can be spoken; the key is *how* to communicate that content.

There will be moments when intuitive information can be called simply what it is and your team can gather to corroborate, modify, or refute what might appear to you to be a truly valuable insight. Over time you may be able to become more direct that what you are communicating stems from gut feeling and then say, "Let's check this out."

- **How does my fantasy or self-interest distort the information?**

Intuitive information is no different from any other kind of information when it comes to bias and self-interest. If I were a 96 year old convinced that a 30-year-old celebrity had fallen madly in love with me, it would be quite easy to discern that I might be living in a fantasy world. If, on the other hand, I were convinced that our company's new product line would be the best thing since the invention of the wheel or the discovery of fire, then charts and projections might belie the likelihood that this new product line would be as much a fantasy as the dreams of that apparently silly person. Once again we return to the axiom, "garbage in, garbage out." Fantasy and self-interest can lead to heartfelt but well-intentioned distortion; it can also lead to simple manipulation and untruths. Discernment is key.

In one organization I worked for I was aware of unethical behavior on the part of another member of the executive management team. What would have been the appropriate response to such a situation? What, if anything, should I report and to whom? The fact that there are often traditional rivalries between these organizational divisions would mean that my reporting a potential problem based on intuitive information would most likely be met with expectations of bias, even if I felt the information to be accurate and considered myself to be serving the organization. As it turned out, I was fortunate to have been given a very personal and internal "heads up" regarding a potential problem, and eventually told my superior to "watch his back." It took another two years before this intuitive information was fully corroborated. My hunch turned out to be correct, but my own self-interest as an individual, and as head of a "rival" division would naturally make me suspect. In situations such as this the best thing to do is to keep one's own counsel, then perhaps to float a trial balloon in the direction of one who could manage the potential problem at an appropriate moment, then duck. There is no reason to be self-righteous or frustrated, because natural rivalries and vested interest make intuitive and any other kind of information suspect. That is why skillful questions, focus, discernment, and integrity are key to the appropriate use of intuitive information, not only in business situations, but also in all of life.

The importance of intention in framing the question: making time vs. "making *time!*"

I was living in Santa Fe, New Mexico, and was scheduled to see clients in Denver, which for several years had become an annual routine. The trip consisted of the usual six-hour drive up Interstate 25. As was my unfortunate bad habit at the time, I was barely getting out the door in time to make my appointments and found myself saying out loud, "I really want to make time on this trip." Making time is fairly common slang in the African-American community, meaning to hurry up and get there fast. Much to my chagrin, however, I *literally* made time: what normally would take six hours to drive took twelve hours! There was no traffic, no additional delay or stops, and there were no accidents on the road. It was, in all regards, a normal trip. But somehow I ended up forgetting about the plasticity of time in my metaphysical worldview, tossed out a quick slang comment, and literally *doubled* the time it took to get there! I literally *made* time!

Deeper intention must be clear when framing a question, or you could find yourself like me: doing what I said, but not what I meant. I literally made more time, when what I wanted to do was hurry up and get there.

Framing a question for intuitive response is high art. There are tips and tricks to framing questions so you can get the most out of the information.

I am a big fan of open-ended questions because I can throw in the kitchen sink and include peripheral matters that might have an important but overlooked effect on the current situation. On the other hand, if the question is too diffuse I might end up with imprecise generalized information and sound like a "woo-woo" psychic.

Quantitative analysts probably prefer questions that make coding and consistency easier to accomplish. If someone wanted to test my ESP abilities, for example, the test might involve my being able to tell which card or suit in a deck would come up next. Or I might be asked a yes-no question such as, "Will the market go up or down next week?" Those tests certainly test something, and they are extremely valuable in computing probabilities. They may also build a bridge between scientific and non-scientific worlds or worldviews. I understand what the quantitative analysts are attempting to do, and I think I understand as well what they are missing. With all my real-world experience and success as an intuitive, I would certainly flunk such a test. Few of life's questions or situations can be framed so neatly. However, if the same researcher were to ask me to tell her about Mary Jones in Oshkosh whom I could not possibly know, I'd be off and running in a second without hesitation and with great specificity. What in the world is *that*?

One of my favorite open-ended intuitive questions is, "What is the one thing I need to know about X?" X could be a person, product, company, meeting, danger, or opportunity. Another might be, "What action, if any, should X take with respect to Y?" Or, "What one piece of advice would I give this CEO or company?" Or even, "How will this venture, partnership, or product turn out in five years?"

My best and most enduring relationships with clients occur when they figure out how to ask me questions that really capture what they mean to find out. When working with a list of priorities it is important to ask, for example, whether number one in the rank order has to do with the most important person or whether number one is an option to *keep* or to *eliminate*. Once the question comes out and it is unclear what the priorities are for, I get confused and have to back off from the question for a time to "clear the palate," so to speak. Sometimes this need to switch away only requires a few moments; sometimes it could take a lot longer. Being clear that this is a list of keep possibilities instead of eliminate possibilities is extremely important. If you are playing intuition games with your staff, you must remember this as well. If the intent of the questions is muddled, you might need to stop and regroup, or go to another issue and later return to the one that was confusing in order to get a clear read on the situation. If you cannot get past the confusion, then ask somebody else to rank order by number without knowing the subject matter at all.

Focus:
That and Only That

I was teaching an intuition workshop in a beautiful rural setting in Austria. The morning of the second day we all stood out on the balcony together, looking at the splendor of the summer fields before us in the early light. Each participant had to select one spot in that field and focus only on that spot. No matter what anyone else selected, or what we thought had been selected by others, or any of the other possible spots we could have chosen, our minds had to go to the very first spot and hold to it for five minutes. We were surrounded with such beauty that focus could be challenging. "That and only that." Hold the thought, the gaze, the intention only on that place in this incredibly unified field of beauty and possible choices for focus. That was a powerful moment. We were each lost in individual focus and reverie, and yet the sense of shared experience was palpable. We could feel the entire field shimmer in delight from our deeper seeing of it.

Accurate business intuition requires a similar ability. There is such beauty and possibility all around (and sometimes fear and danger), that maintaining clear and unswerving focus can be difficult. But focus is the practice, the skill to be learned. In this way you avoid distortion and confusion and you improve accuracy.

There are lots of simple techniques to improve focus. Many meditation practices develop such abilities. If you are too busy or prefer not to engage in formal meditation, simply finding a spot on the wall in your office during the workday and staring at it or five minutes could increase your focus dramatically. That and only that. Staring at a candle flame is another good technique, especially since the flame is in constant motion, changing form and color. If you find your mind wandering, remind yourself of focus by noticing aspects of the flame: how it moves and changes color. Use your curiosity about the flame to keep you focused on it and nothing else for five minutes. An auxiliary benefit of this simple exercise will be ending the mental break with a clearer head, prepared for the next round of challenges. Or, forgetting about the challenges for five minutes, you may come to notice that they were not so insurmountable after all. Five minutes may seem like a long time, but you will be amazed to see how different you feel once you focus. You may notice new things in your everyday surroundings.

If your workplace provides little privacy, take a few moments longer in the bathroom and stare at a place on the stall wall or floor. This suggestion might sound yucky, but when you focus and notice the sheen of the paint or the pattern of the tile, you can actually come away with renewed concentration and a sense of ease.

One type of intuitive situation is particularly fraught with mix-ups. A client may have three children, and before I can stop him he is rattling off the names of all three. I may get confused: is the person thinking of his children in birth order, order of affection or problematic behavior, or alphabetical order? (There goes that rational mind again!) It is hard to focus on only one child when all the names are thrown out in a jumble. If possible, I will catch the client and say something like, "Tell me the names of your children *one at a time*. Just give me one name, and we'll look at the others later." This question about children often introduces confusion. I have had the experience of completely missing the description of the child the client asked about first, only to find a few moments later that I was describing in great detail the person's other child! Sometimes one name just stands out, even though I don't know the children at all. On other occasions it is the parent who has not seen the child as he or she really is, and the child he thinks to be one way is quite the other. This is another reason the seven-second rule is so important: say a name, start speaking immediately, and then trust and hold to what you receive.

Reliability

H oned, developed intuition is more reliable than either pure reason or pure gut alone. Reliability in the domain of intuitive information has three principal areas of focus: the reliability of the source of the information; the reliability of the information itself; and the assurance that any subsequent information received will be as reliable as the first. While there is overlap among these considerations, establishing confidence in the credibility of the source of intuitive data appears to be more important than establishing the credibility of the source of numerical data. Neither is free from subjective influence.

If I tell you that my intuitive information derives from an insight I had while reading a book on management, it is likely that you will at least pay some attention to what I say. If I tell you that my information—the exact same information—derives from a space being from the twelfth dimension, it is unlikely you will give me a moment's notice. In this case the issue is not the reliability of the information *itself*, which might sound quite reasonable, but the *source* of that information, which may or may not appear to be credible and reasonable. How can I consider a space being from a twelfth dimension to be a reliable source of intuitive data for the success of my very practical business, when I know of only three dimensions and do not believe in extraterrestrial intelligence? Even if the information could make the company rich, I would resist any attempt to risk the well being of my company on such an apparently unreliable source.

How can intuitive information be credible in a business environment? How does the information rise above the label of "fortune telling?"

I remember meeting with another group of CEOs to offer an intuition workshop. The host of the meeting had apparently decided in advance that what I did was not intuition, but "clairvoyance" and "fortune telling." He clearly held deep beliefs about what he believed to be evil, and set about to sabotage the workshop before it had even begun. What a difficult experience! No amount of explanation on my part could salvage this extremely uncomfortable situation. If an individual believes that intuition is nothing more than fortune telling, there is nothing more to do or say. The doors of possibility and perception are closed and will remain so, whether the workshop lasts for a day or a decade. I moved on after a very strained encounter, clear that there was no room for curiosity in the company run by that particular CEO at that time.

Belief in the source typically makes people believe in the data. The violation of trust felt when a trusted source is found to be either corrupt or just plain faulty can be quite intense, and can incur not only appropriate wrath, but hefty fines as well. It took years of cumulative data to make investors aware that perhaps their trusted sources of financial data were faulty at best and absolutely wrong at the height of the significant downturn in financial markets. There were countless clues from intuitive sources that something fairly fundamental to the structuring of global financial instruments was afoot, but because the intuitive sources were considered unreliable, and traditional sources had not yet discerned new patterns emerging, many people lost their livelihood as businesses failed or were greatly devalued.

When is that magic moment when the source of information must be questioned deeply, even if it has been reliable in the past? How do we recognize fundamental structural changes on the horizon before they wipe out investments and savings? In truth, the source and content of information should be questioned at every moment and at every level. One must never be lulled to sleep by past patterns, whether mainstream or intuitive. How can we learn to question without becoming immobilized or unable to trust at all?

Intuition helps trigger an internal awareness that it is time to pay closer attention; it is an internal alarm that permits routine action, pending some personal signal that the information received is no longer reliable. The signal is simply a trigger for increased awareness that may or may not be related to specific investments or stock performance. It can be expressed as a bodily sensation; the synchronous appearance of "signs" such as arrows or repeating numbers in the environment, or other individualized clues. For example, you might mentally see the face of your broker with his or her head hanging or tucked into the overcoat. This would be a good time for a phone call to ask, "How are things going?" During the next few weeks you might pay special attention to the market until you feel you can coast again.

Gut feeling, while often considered unreliable, can be of great service when traditional sources of data fail. Once investors have already taken significant losses based on rational analysis, the presumably greater risk of seeking out intuitive data when all else has failed is no longer such a big deal. This is a moment for thinking outside the box, for discovering whether information from an intuitive source can make a difference in current performance and future earnings. On the other hand, thinking outside the box when all was going well might have served even *better*!

Replicability

Replicability in intuitive experiments poses different challenges compared to what would normally be required in rational experiments. Each intuitive situation is different and can never be replicated precisely. The variables change and the probabilities shift in a nanosecond, even for the same individual, or commodity, or business, or financial market. For my intuitive purposes, replicability means I can "nail" a situation over and over, not that the situation itself is the same. Measures must be established to assess this type of continuously changing "intuition on the fly," all the while understanding that no two people or situations will ever be intuitively the same.

During the mid 1990s I worked with a British physicist whom I will call Ian, and a social scientist I will call Alex, on informal telepathic experiments we called the Thought Form Project (TFP). During the same period of time I worked briefly with another well-known scientist on a series of remote viewing experiments. The remote viewing experiments required rigid protocols and double blind studies; the target was not actually selected until *after* the viewing experiment was over! The Thought Form Project, on the other hand, permitted far more leeway because we were playful in our work together. While less replicable, our informal work permitted more surprise and raised more questions for further research than the selection of photographs from a set of probable choices. For the TFP, we were not limited with regard to the information we would send or receive; we could select literally *anything* in our physical environment for focus. The result was consistent and rather remarkable "hits," even though the experiment was impossible to replicate.

Ian and I lived 5,000 miles apart at the time. One afternoon I decided to sit on the ground in my back yard in Santa Fe and look between the spokes on my bicycle tire. Ian sent back a hand-drawn image of my *entire back yard,* as if it had been taken from an aerial view just over the garage. The rendering was perfect, but certainly not replicable. I expected to see a round image with lines, or perhaps the wooden wall on the other side of the bicycle through which I was peering seated on the ground. But what I received was a correct drawing of a much larger space.

I could claim that what he saw was "wrong," because his image did not match my specific and literal viewpoint. On the other hand, what he saw was even better, and to my thinking supremely more accurate than my limited view through those tire spokes.

As businesses move through an ever-changing landscape, it is critical to develop new measures for determining the validity and replicability of intuitive information. The fact that our experiments were neither scientifically replicable nor mathematically reliable in no way meant they were uninteresting or invalid. In our own playful way, we received important hits every week that were far beyond chance. In addition, some of our most remarkable information came when we were not focused officially on the task for that week.

On one occasion we were to connect at the usual time on Monday. That week, however, my daughter had become ill and was admitted to the hospital. I was so focused on her well being that I forgot to email Ian to let him know we would not be meeting telepathically as planned.

He thought we were doing the experiment, so he wrote down impressions at the normally agreed upon time. This time, however, he was quite confused and sent his results in with a set of puzzling comments. "I never get images like these," he said. "I can't figure out what was going on with me this week. This is so bizarre; I never seem to get oriental images." And then he began to describe something like a display involving oriental art or figures. What in the world was that?

It so happens that at the time my colleague Ian had focused on me, I was sitting in a Chinese restaurant adjacent to the hospital while we waited for news on my daughter's condition. We had been at the hospital for hours and had not eaten all day, so finally we went next door to grab a bite to eat.

The person Ian described in his email to me matched precisely the woman who seemed to own the restaurant and who was serving us. At the table where we were sitting, I was facing the check-out counter, beneath which mannequin-like figures in traditional dress were placed on display. It was as if Ian were looking out through my eyes in the restaurant! I had forgotten about our usual session because my focus was on my daughter, but he went on with it anyway and connected unilaterally. Or, somewhere in the back of my conscious awareness, I did think about Ian and let him in to share my experience.

No planned experiment could have achieved the success Ian achieved with this impromptu session. Had we not already established a habit of focusing our thoughts and writing down what we got, this story might never have come to light. The "missed" appointment turned out to be one of our most interesting experiments! There is so much more to learn about the relationship between telepathy and intuition. We are just at the beginning.

Margins of error

What, then, is an acceptable margin of error for intuitive information for business applications? Unfortunately, the answer at this point is, "I don't know." We must conduct much more research before analysis yields reliable answers. Of this I am certain, however: intuition for business applications in my own work is far beyond what could reasonably be called chance or luck. Furthermore, clients and companies seem to be benefitting, so something must be sufficiently reliable to earn mutual trust and loyalty.

Tackling the Validity Issue
for Intuitive Information

One of my business clients was interested in only a few narrowly focused commodities. I had worked with this client at least once a week, and sometimes more often, over the course of two years or more. While not every prediction was correct, he began to notice that the *pattern* of trading I was giving him intuitively was on the mark, but the *timing* for the pattern to become fully expressed was off the mark. Make no mistake about it: timing is critical, and I will have more to say about that. We also discovered that I did much better with long-term predictions than short-term ones, precisely the opposite of weather forecasters.

It can be a daunting task to prove the validity of intuitive information to such a sufficient degree that individuals and companies are willing to make decisions and invest tremendous resources on a business hunch, especially *before* the benefit of hindsight proves the hunch to have been correct. Nevertheless, investors are willing to make what is the equivalent of "bets" on the future through commodities trading. They may see mounds of analyses, historical information, trends, charts, graphs, numbers, and the advice of their own professional intuitives, otherwise known as hedge fund managers or stockbrokers. Ultimately, however, they are all trading on a hunch as well.

It is the very role of intuition to provide information that makes no rational sense at the time, and to add that "non-rational" information to other sources provided in the usual, rational and quantitative ways.

Validity can only be established *ex post facto*. While there are measures for predicting that a certain event or set of probabilities will occur, there can be no true tests ahead of time for the *validity* of precognitive information, or for its inherent quality. This does not mean, however, that intuitive information is therefore useless or pointless. For intuitive information, qualitative and unobtrusive measures are a must. What ultimately turns out to be valid information remains valuable, even though it may not meet objective quantitative standards. Hitting the price of oil is a concrete test of validity. Replicating that success beyond chance is a bit trickier: only time and experience will tell. Eventually a pattern of hits will emerge. Furthermore, hitting the benefit of a strategic partnership in the present may require many more measures and analyses to determine validity one or five or ten years later. Intuition can go out that far in a blink.

The proof of the pudding is in the eating; the proof of valid intuitive information, of the hunch, is in its corroboration. What *can* be measured is the percentage of times a particular manager or professional intuitive is correct, has a "hit:" for example, predicts where the currency market will be on a particular date and time. What *cannot* be measured is the value and validity of intuitive information that is not numbers driven: "How will this restructuring affect the overall effectiveness of this organization?" We can attempt to attach productivity percentages to employee performance, for example, but that percentage is not a measure of the validity of the intuitive information that initially drove the restructuring process or convinced the CEO of the need for significant overhaul. Since I often work without access to privileged information, the mainstream news is interestingly enough my best source of corroboration. That, plus the fact that those clients come back for more intuitive information and support, even when they cannot share with me exactly how the information has impacted policy decisions.

Measuring the effectiveness of intuitive information can be challenging in so many ways. Just as it is impossible to determine the effectiveness of government agencies in thwarting terrorist attacks, it is equally difficult to determine the impact of intuitive support on successful business decisions. Often there is no feedback: for a variety of reasons the government would not or could not tell the general population how many attempts were actually carried out to threaten our sense of security. There is also the so-called observer effect in the domain of intuition: the fact that someone gives advance notice about certain probable occurrences changes the outcomes. How much of the change in a positive direction came from the intuitive information proffered, and how much from other totally unrelated factors? It is impossible to know with absolute certainty. One can only pay attention to patterns and try to make sense out of clues.

Following the World Trade Center events in 2001 I agreed to send intuitive information to the FBI through a colleague regarding potential events in New York, Chicago and Texas. I knew it was unlikely I would ever hear back for confirmation or denial; I just figured that if the information proved useful I would have done my small part. I will never know if anything I told them (distorted perhaps by the need for third party communication) ever proved useful. There have been some vague public statements about agencies that successfully thwarted terrorist attempts; who knows whether intuitive information contributed to that success? I certainly do not, even if such information would increase my "validity score."

Another challenge related to the issue of validity is isolating the impact of the intuitive information alone in a multifaceted and complex organization, where decision making occurs simultaneously on many levels by individuals who may or may not be involved consciously in intuitive practices. Larry Dossey highlights this problem when he writes about the difficulty of measuring the effect of prayer on healing.[9] Researchers were able to establish control groups and prayer groups fairly easily. What stymied them, however, was their inability to determine or control who was praying for patients *on their own*, completely apart from the prayer studies. They discovered that other people had been praying for the patient as well. How could they tell that the patient's improved health was the result of the prayer group's intervention and not all those others who voluntarily prayed without being specifically asked to do so? How can we tell whether the success of a particular venture or corporate intervention is the result of the information provided by the *intuitive*, or by some other relevant organizational processes? At some point, the effective use of intuition depends upon detaching from the outcome, ignoring for the moment how valid it will show itself to be in the future. Unlike other objective measures, I have learned as a professional intuitive that the more detached I remain from the need to prove, the more accurate and valid the results.

When intuitive information proves to be a key factor in the success of a particular decision or event or outcome, those involved will feel the impact, regardless of what is stated publicly at a later time. They will know and will return to use such awareness again. Even if the power of intuitive tools can never be fully claimed in an overt way, intuition has no personality or ego that suffers from lack of acknowledgment. On the other hand, employees suffer when their work goes unrecognized or undervalued. It is the very nature of intuition to be serving humanity from the hidden corners of consciousness. Like the sun, which rises whether or not we forget to thank it each day, intuition remains a constant companion as well, waiting for us to turn inward and welcome it.

Integrity
What Goes Around Comes Around

When Robert's colleagues tried to discern what his new product was in my earlier example, their intention was not to harm or "get him;" it was to help him and themselves. Fortunately they had jelled as a group before our session, so the CEO who volunteered could have reasonable certainty that his colleagues would not betray any privileged information. The goal of intuitive information is to enhance collaboration, support optimal expression, and recognize the good intention lurking in the shadows of ostensibly adversarial relationships. Intuition is a survival tool, as Laura Day expressed in her book *Practical Intuition*,[10] but it is not a Machiavellian tool to conquer someone else before being conquered. It is a way to discover the best outcome for all involved from the present vantage point.

The belief in finite resources is strong, especially in the business world. As a result the tendency is to forgive ethical lapses if one is perceived to be serving the greater good of the company by gobbling up resources without thinking about the consequences for others. Ultimately, however, the chickens come home to roost. There are intuitive ways to keep tabs on company ethics and priorities.

Think about the company you own or manage. Would you be willing to work in any position in that business? How much do you know about each and every component of your production cycle, whether what you produce is goods, services, software, or connections?

You may not be able to make it physically to every nook and cranny of your operation, but through intuitive Q & A you can rank order what needs to be addressed and resolved on a daily basis, and you can identify the best candidates to make it so. You can remain in integrity with those who support and benefit from your success. You *must* remain in integrity with your customers, employees, managers, community, adversaries, and ultimately yourself.

We all have a responsibility to use information in an ethical manner. A businessman I know had a habit of developing special relationships with women in his rivals' divisions. He would use the women to gather and report information for a grand takeover scheme. The women would comply because they enjoyed the special attention of this charismatic figure (were they being ignored by their direct supervisor?). Had this executive realized that all divisions of the company are connected anyway, and that there was no need for subterfuge to know what was going on, he might have saved himself some "comes around" consequences. He was subsequently fired for unethical behavior.

Intuitive information, which is often highly sensitive, comes with special responsibilities. If I get an intuitive hit that someone I work with and care about is going through difficulties at home or facing medical problems, what do I do with that information? Do I tell co-workers, who might begin to avoid that person like the plague? Do I say something on the side to somebody in the human resources office, threatening a potential loss of employment and benefits when the person is most vulnerable?

Sometimes all is takes is a moment to stop, give the person a warm, sincere, direct look in the eye, and ask, "How are you doing?" And then you must slow down long enough to actually wait for a reply. Often the person might not want to talk, but sometimes just the moment of acknowledgement is enough to keep him or her going for a while.

Let's return to the case of Matthew: when partnership negotiations were going on, it turned out to be an important bit of intuitive information that the chief negotiator was about to leave the company. Already suffering from "short-timer's disease," he wanted to get the negotiation completed as quickly as possible. We didn't know if this individual had even signaled to his bosses that he was about to go. The intuitive information was useful to my client, but there was no need to broadcast that tidbit to anybody else, either in my client's company or the company entering into negotiation with him. Matthew and I were the only ones who discussed this. Negotiations ended successfully and favorably for my client, and the negotiator did leave the other company. That was enough to know.

There are some pretty simple rules of conduct for the ethical use of intuitive information in the workplace. Most are just plain common sense and good business practice if you want to stay out of court or jail. But when you have access to privileged information, it is more important than ever to stay on your ethical track.

Whole Life a Prayer

In preparation to teach intuition to a group of executives at a well-known executive training program, the founder of the program asserted during his presentation that if an intuitive does not begin a consultation with a prayer, then the information itself would not be reliable, and the source of the information could not be trusted. Sitting in the back of the room, I mulled over that assertion for a while, feeling a bit taken aback.

The man who spoke is one of the great minds in the field of business intuition and a most extraordinary human being on every level. When we met during the break I asked him about his statement requiring prayer at the beginning of each consultation. "What if your *whole life* is a prayer?" I asked.

I consider my entire life, warts and all, to be in its very essence a prayer. To say it in a slightly different and more secular way, the very purpose of my work is to enhance the well being and success of those with whom I work. For me to stop and pray at the beginning of a consultation could infer that in other moments I might *not* be focused on good intention, or the accuracy of information and the well being of the other person. On the other hand, taking that moment to center and to be present for the client serves an important purpose, assuring and reassuring the integrity of the intuitive process. Each of us must decide what works best for us and follow that impulse without wavering. The centering moment could be a prayer, a single breath, a more elaborate ritual you prefer, or a simple looking into the eyes of the person sitting across from you, whether client, customer, or employee.

I believe that in spite of the daunting facts, the human experience rests on a foundation of good intention, no matter how distorted that impulse sometimes becomes.

PART TWO

Seven Second Decision Making In Key Areas Of Business

The Seven Second Guide to Mergers and Strategic Partnerships

Be sure who you are as a company first

You cannot negotiate anything, including a strategic partnership or merger, if you do not know who you are and what you want to achieve from the negotiation process. Every training document says so. Being caught up in the panic or excitement of a potential merger or strategic partnership, you may be too close to the action to perceive fully all you need to know in order to make this potential relationship a success. You can get short answers in seven seconds or less as you plan for this important new transition, whether or not you welcome the change. You can discover potential allies, who may not be the key players at the negotiating table. You can also discover who might be out to sabotage this deal, not only on the other team, but also on your own team as well. Using seven second "hits" to get the name or initials of parties to be concerned about can make all the difference in the world when you are in the thick of things. By framing strategic questions about your and what you perceive to be the other party's bottom line, you can begin to answer the essence of these questions in seven seconds or less. In this way you get to the heart of the matter without having to go through a protracted thought process.

You can always develop your response to deeper and more complex questions over time, based partly on intuition and partly on other traditional business support tools. Remember that the intuitive information you garner is simply one tool to help you frame a partnership that is fulfilling to both parties. It utilizes all of your prior experience and training in that millisecond of processing; and it incorporates matters of both head and heart easily and quickly, so you can bring the whole self and the whole company to the table.

If you welcome the change and are desperate, for example, thinking you may be finally getting out from under the financial and structural burden of running a struggling company, you might see *any* partner as welcomed. You might tend to ignore signals about the potential partner's intention concerning the acquisition or merger. Such thinking assumes that you believe you and the company no longer have substantial value and you push the partnership through before being "found out."

If you resist the change, even if the acquiring or merging entity "walks on water," you may have a hard time knowing the true value of the potential partnership. No matter what is said or done on the surface of things, selecting the most fulfilling of probabilities requires an intuitive boost.

In either case intuition helps you thread your way through potential minefields as you settle ultimately on that perfect business partner, whether that partner is a single individual or a giant company.

Find out who "they" are institutionally and personally ahead of time

It is important to avoid engaging in an "us" and "them" mentality. Even if the partnership is desired, there is often a tendency to pit us against them. "Who are they? What do they really want? Will they manipulate us, exploit us, and take advantage of our company?"

Use your intuition to go to that place that is detached from the outcome: perhaps this is the right partner, perhaps not. Ask questions intuitively, not only about their good intention, but also about whether or not this partnership can work, regardless of their initial intention.

Use the name of the company itself first. Write it down, speak it to someone, discuss it as a group. The company's name carries meaning encoded in concentrated form through word and image. What is the fundamental identity of the company? When you know the identity of the company, including its mission and future, then you can go down the detailed list of parties to the negotiation or the potential blended company.

It is possible that the fit between your company and the other one is strong, but there may be a blockage at the level of leadership based on personality or structural issues. There may also be competition between senior partners or managers in the other company, or your own. You may be dealing with someone who wants the partnership to work, and be unaware that this person is engaged in a lock-horns battle with another senior executive who does not wish for the partnership to take place.

You can retrieve such information intuitively. First try to detach emotionally from your current relationship with that entity and take a look. Perhaps you will get an image, a symbol, a word, a phrase. There are business consultants who work with companies to develop their institutional metaphor. Perhaps you get a metaphor. Ask the question, "Who or what is the essence of this company?"

This exercise may indicate that there is no true fit between this company and yours, even if good intention and interest abound between both parties. As you look at the company itself and its core business, you may discover that you are trying to force a shoe made for someone else on a foot that does not fit.

If the images you receive from this exercise are positive, keep going. "They are committed to excellence; they are providing a niche market with a particular good or service. Their product or service may be the same as ours, so it is not a stretch for them to enter into partnership with us." Or, "We bring to their core mission an expansion or diversification that requires minimal retooling. This can work."

Perhaps your companies are quite different; for example, the potential strategic partner franchises food or beverages. You may own a trucking company. The F&B business depends upon trucks to distribute its products to its franchisees. Being in different businesses does not necessarily limit a beneficial partnership. That potential partner's business has now grown from one to twenty-five stores, and the company is tired of leasing vehicles from trucking companies. It has decided to acquire its own fleet of vehicles. This could be an excellent partnership.

Here are some simple tools to help prepare for that meeting or negotiation. You can add specific questions related to your company's interests or special domain, of course. You can also add questions related to the participation of members of your Board of Directors and shareholders who may not be present in the room while you talk things out, but who could influence your negotiations in significant ways.

Remember, this is a list of questions to ask *intuitively*. You may have many more complicated structural and legal documents that you will use at the table; these questions are to help you prepare before you get to the table and during breaks.

Managing Meetings and Negotiations

- Who is attending from my company or division, and what do I need to know about each person *relevant to the meeting*?
- Who is deciding, whether present or absent?
- What is my right team mix?
- Who is the other company or party sending to the meeting?
- How will the meeting or negotiation go?
- What should I communicate, and to whom, following the meeting?
- What is my responsibility in this meeting and following it?
- Is there a number or percentage or outcome that will make me consider the negotiation a success?
- What is the single most important thing that could derail this process?
- What is going to surprise me today?

Who Will Be There?

Name	One Thing I Need To Know
1. _____	_____
2. _____	_____
3. _____	_____
4. _____	_____
5. _____	_____
6. _____	_____
7. _____	_____

Sometimes the other party will not provide a list of who will be present. If not, then you can look up basic information about the company and guess intuitively who will be there. You might even ask someone who is not privy to the other party's information to play the intuitive game with you on this round, and throw out some initials that simply pop into his or her head. The key always is to get the rational mind out of the way so deeper information can seep into your waking awareness. Once it does, you are free to use all the usual tools and tricks of your particular trade to optimize what you have learned intuitively in ethical ways.

Most importantly, the list of questions elicits information about the influence of *absent and unnamed* parties or interests. Intuition is a terrific aid in seeing around corners and behind the back, and in avoiding ambush in public settings.

Trucking Food

A trucking company has been looking for a major anchor client and is tired of looking for individual contracts of limited financial gain. They imagine that landing a single huge contract with a company like McDonald's or Burger King or yours might solve all its problems.

However, there may be senior executives or partners in your business, the franchise food business, who feel it either premature or unwise to acquire your own fleet of trucks. You expect hidden costs having to do with maintenance, motor pools, insurance, and driver benefits, which normally the trucking company would cover. They might also feel that this kind of hardware acquisition would be unwise and could put a strain on the needs of your core business. You are concerned with cooking, heating and refrigeration hardware, rather than with the trucks that would carry the hardware. The trucking company might want to keep cargo-flexible trucks and not outfit them with the costly heating, storage, and ventilation capability that trucking food requires. On the other hand, perhaps the trucks themselves become the very heating and refrigeration devices you are seeking!

Someone in your company will have to determine the true cost of partnering or seeking an outright acquisition of the trucking company. Even if you agree internally on the numbers, you may disagree on their rank order of priorities. It is possible, for example, that your investors and managers might consider it more important to invest in refrigerated airplanes, or in a refrigeration company as an auxiliary to your core business rather than in a fleet of trucks. They might even want to invest in a slaughterhouse or farm or dairy or bottling company. All of these are potential options for your franchise food and beverage business. Why should you acquire or partner with a trucking company?

You can be certain that there will be many discussions in the Board and executive conference rooms around these issues, as there should be. Adding intuition to these discussions saves an enormous amount of time and money, ultimately shoring up the bottom line.

As a senior executive you can frame the following questions, and then answer them first in *seven seconds or less* off the top of your head:

- Of the possible diversification options for our company, which is the one that best suits our current and near future needs? You could frame this as an open-ended question first.

Alternatively, you could develop a list of already discussed diversification options, rank order the list, and then ask an open-ended question about the option that pops us as your number one priority: "Why is this the best option?"

- Of the possible strategic partnerships, which company and which leaders do we get along with best, whether in the trucking industry or not? Why do we get along so well with them?

- Of the possible acquisitions we could make, which would be the most cost-effective for this period of time?

- Of the choices we might make, which will have the greatest hidden costs five, ten, twenty years down the road? Given the recent acceleration of change cycles, especially in the domains of technology and financial services industries, the long term could be a mere twelve months ahead! Too often companies make strategic decisions from a short-term perspective: five-year plans are typically the range, instead of thirty or fifty years. For non-profits, surpassing the ten-year mark usually determines the life or death of the organization. The longer view is more reflective of company life cycles and neighborhood turnaround.

- If we know we wish to diversify and acquire or partner with a trucking company and we have interest on the part of ABC Trucking, is this the best trucking company relationship to pursue at this time? A simple intuitive "Yes," "No," or "Maybe" is enough to begin. A clear and compelling "No!" might be sufficient to stop you in your tracks. The next question, of course, would be why the "No!" was so strong. "What are we missing?"

- Is there another trucking company on the horizon that we would be better suited to discover?

- What is the optimal period of time for entering into such a partnership? Is it now, as soon as we can complete this negotiation? Is it later? If so, how much later?

These are all questions that can be answered *initially and intuitively* more effectively than all those hours of wrangling in the Board Room. The seven seconds technique helps you shape questions for deeper discussion, data analysis, research, and timing, and sets the framework for various workgroups.

Look ahead: will this partnership work in the long run?

While scenario planning and computer simulations look into the future to see what the blended partnership will have become in two, five, ten, or twenty years, nothing accomplishes this as well as applied intuition. Given the acceleration of change, those time periods become increasingly compressed, so that managers often take to looking month-to-month instead of year over year.

Whatever the time frame, it is literally possible to see who will still be there, who will have left, who will be the person or persons with true influence and authority in the company, and who will engage in what kinds of power struggles with whom. All of this is based, of course, on current configurations and most likely outcomes, other things being equal. You are not dealing with fate; on the other hand, you have the gift of the current moment to see the most likely probabilities and outcomes. With the information that derives from this inspired knowing, you are able to make adjustments along the way with a greater amount of ease than if likely events were not known to you in advance. Intuition diminishes unwanted surprise.

You can find out whether or not promises and agreements you made in the creation of this partnership will be honored in the future. The way intuition works in general is that at any point in time you are able to see the most likely outcome, given the structure, parties, and issues when the questions are framed. As you make successive decisions and move along in this process, free will always comes into play and scenarios inevitably change.

Refined and appropriate use of intuition allows you to act, refrain from acting, or modify your actions in light of the information you receive from any source. You may look ahead and see that about three years out there will be difficulties with the partnership. These difficulties will occur with individuals X, A, and F who are current players in the formation of this new blended company. You can forestall, change, avoid, or improve the foreseen outcomes because of the intuitive heads up.

Sometimes challenges result from structural problems that were unanticipated consequences of the new partnership. Issues emerge because those members of the business who were "acquired" or blended into a larger company exhibit increasingly low morale, bitterness, and regret that they engaged in this partnership in the first place. Thus there are efforts to undermine the partnership and the business, even when undermining affects their personal security.

Sometimes the problems arise not with the company that is acquired or the "old" leadership, but with broken promises of the new leadership. Employees on both sides begin to feel like second-class citizens: they are unacknowledged, moved out of former assignments, and given less authority without being terminated. New leaders renege on prior agreements once the partnership is formalized. This results in ill will and possible outright sabotage. It is important to have that inspired look into the future to know which areas worked really well and which areas did not work. Then you can adjust actions, agreements, and settlements *in the present moment* that will head off those potential *foreseen* problems in the future. Unforeseen moments will continue to occur, of course, but intuition helps diminish these circumstances.

The goal always is good intention and success. No one would consciously choose failure as an option. When employees or managers get really angry, they may *appear* to choose failure for a fleeting moment because of their unhappiness. But a failed company means *everybody* is out of work and that disgruntled employee receives no income or benefits. It is important to look beneath the surface of any unhappiness and find the true issue or intention, which is never failure, even if it appears to be so in the heat of the moment.

Assume the food and beverage company and the trucking company have indeed blended. Look into the future and see the actual impact of the decision. For example, what is the impact on the bottom line of the company by owning this component of its distribution chain as compared to leasing? What are the unanticipated positive or negative consequences? Most especially, what are the *surprises*, whether positive or negative? How has the merger helped the success of both components, formerly both companies? It is possible to start receiving information on these matters *in advance* in seven seconds or less.

What is the next change or new market niche for this blended or partnered company?

Once the partnership is completed with great success, the task of new management is to determine now, even before the transition phase is completed, what the next opportunity or change will be for the blended company.

Perform both rational and intuitive SWOT analyses, beginning with the intuitive: strengths, weaknesses, opportunities, and threats.[11] "The company has acquired a trucking division to add to its food and beverage franchise. When will there be an appropriate moment, if ever, for us to launch into direct production of cattle or restaurant equipment—or the acquisition of real estate?"

In order for a large chain such as McDonald's to create recognizable spaces in each community where a franchise was located, the company had to become involved in the real estate business. It had to identify appropriate locations for a new franchise, acquire lots, and construct buildings that were designed according to a template. At some point real estate became at least as important for the large chain as the production of food and beverage. The Howard Johnson chain faced similar challenges decades ago, and fared less well with market fluctuations after an extended period of success. When the company begins to sell or lease these franchises to other individuals, it must become deeply involved in new areas: landlord-tenant relations and entrepreneurial training, as well as product and service management. Existing employees may be highly experienced in the food, beverage, hospitality, and restaurant management aspects of the business, but there may be no current staff highly qualified in real estate. Owners end up creating new divisions of the company and hiring a new genre of employee.

"Yes, we produce food and beverages; yes we lease certain equipment and own certain equipment; yes, we have now added a trucking business to assist us in our distribution of goods. What will it take now for us to create our own branded buildings?" In the same way that you use your gut feeling to know whether or not this partnership will work, you can identify individuals not currently known to the company who could come in and launch this new effort. They could either head up a new subsidiary engaged in real estate acquisition, construction, and maintenance; or the parent company could spin off a totally new company, wholly owned by the parent company but separate from it.

These are questions, challenges, and opportunities that rely as heavily on inspiration as they do on perspiration, on plain hard work. When is timing good for this new direction? The company may have begun in the 1950's, but it may not be until 1975 or 1980 that the company decides to go full out in the real estate or trucking business. Since time is equidistant in the intuitive worldview, thirty years into the future is as easy to view and assess as the most recent five-year plan.

Perhaps there is another future moment when select products from the restaurant menu are branded and sold in supermarkets. "Take home that special whipped dessert or frozen patty or spicy chicken recipe! Recreate the experience at home if you cannot or do not wish to drive to one of our restaurants." It would be a strategic decision to place certain products in supermarkets—or not. This is another threshold moment in the life of a business or parent company.

When such strategic decisions must be made, intuition really comes in to save the day.

If the company has acquired the trucking business, for example, it would not matter if the trucks were delivering to their own restaurants or to third party supermarkets. The earlier strategic decision to acquire the trucking business would hold over time. On the other hand, if the company made the decision to partner with a supermarket chain and provide these packaged meals to the store in much the same way as they would have done for a franchise, the company might risk losing restaurant customers and risk being left with enormous real estate losses as buildings become empty or underutilized. They might also need to reduce or increase the size of their trucking fleet.

Intuitive decision making tools benefit such strategic decisions because there is no attachment to the outcome in that brief moment outside of time, and no prior action to defend. Use the answers derived from the seven-second process to shape, frame the research, and flesh out your strategic decisions. "How many customers will stay at home if we provide these products through supermarket chains?" And for a different kind of business, "How many banks, bookstores, video store buildings will go under if we provide those services online?" The original intention will be to expand the current business: those who go to branded locations for hot food. On the other hand, those who go to the supermarket instead, stock up, and heat up their food may stay at home and empty our restaurants. The potential risks incurred from enormous investments in real estate to bring the people to you in the first place are apparent. Why would such a company wish to put its products on supermarket shelves? Instead of the intended expansion of its business, the result might be diminished business and increased capital losses because the physical locations are no longer gaining sufficient foot traffic to make them financially viable. The company is then stuck with land, bricks and mortar, which might be difficult to sell because they were constructed in the first place to match the identity of the parent company. Turning such franchises into neutral commercial space could be quite challenging. On the other hand, the company might be wise enough to make its products ubiquitous, whether on the road or at home.

Even at the beginning of creating a franchise, it is possible to answer these questions well in advance if necessary—even decades in advance. In the realm of intuition the future is just next door from the present: looking ahead fifty years is no more challenging than looking ahead five.

Partnership Pitfalls and Pratfalls

Once the strategic decisions have been made, it is relatively easy to identify now any pitfalls or potential problems the partnership will experience down the road. These might be executive management weaknesses, structural problems, cash flow problems, branding challenges, and new niche market opportunities. Even finding the right name can prove to be daunting when history and egos are on the line.

There is no greater tool for identifying the perfect business name than intuition. Should the new name be some combination of the two former company names? Should a third, neutral name be selected that identifies this newly partnered business? Many companies pay enormous sums of money to branding specialists: consultants who will help them identify a new name for the company. The seven-second process can be used to help identify or discover a company name that could work. One way would be to use the tools and lists discussed in this book to consider options. Another would be to mentally travel ten years out, look at the sign over the headquarters of the company, and simply "read" the sign and see what you see affixed there. Of the most likely probabilities, which one was chosen? Does the building look healthy where the sign pops up? Go into the future and read the book not yet written. See the logo *after* it has been created in the future, and then come back and "retro-create" it based on your mental journey. While this may sound like a far-fetched idea, the line between science fiction and science fact becomes increasingly narrow. After all, who knows the true source of DaVinci's aeronautical drawings? Could he have been inspired by future *or even past* flying machines? There is much more to learn about the nature and source of inventiveness.

Another option, of course, would be to engage in routine research and the use of marketing and branding consultants to come up with possible scenarios for graphical identity. Then you could add a twist and use the intuitive tool to choose among those options.

Traditional work could and would be done, of course: the companies or partners could narrow down a list of possible names and graphical identities to ten or five or three choices. They could determine which one will have the greatest impact in seven seconds or less: is it number one or number four? Whatever the number, it is critical to trust that impulse. One of the options could be, "none of the above." Keep looking. One of the numbers could be name X or Y. One of the numbers could be, "You are on to something here; keep working." So your choices would include actual names and perhaps images. The list could also have embedded in it options not yet known. You might have four choices, for example, but find out that a sixth would be better than the four known. Learn from what was created in building the first four to develop the sixth, even better, concept. Because name represents the essential qualities of the company, it is critical that the name itself be well chosen. It must carry with it the infusion of the intention, experience, dreams, wishes, and desires of those parties who are creating this new company.

Avoid any pitfalls or unanticipated consequences that might arise from your partnership or merger. Trust that you can use your gut to recognize the warning signs of partnership or merger failure below in seven seconds or less without knowing how you know.

Partnership Pitfalls and Pratfalls

- o Forgetting who you are
- o Forgetting who they are
- o Resisting inevitable change
- o Refusing to see the handwriting on the wall: time for you to leave personally, or to break up the partnership?
- o Being neither fish nor fowl . . . failing to recognize what partnerships *cannot* fix
- o Resisting the pressure to call a spade a spade: Is this a merger or an acquisition?
- o Underestimating what's in a (new) name
- o Underestimating the cost of war in hostile takeovers: time, money, human and other resources; including the loss of an alternate business opportunity that could have come with greater ease and profit

---

Don't just look now, look out later and see what challenges will present themselves later on, even if everything your gut tells you now says "This is good; go with it." Just because it is good and right now, you want to be prepared for future challenges when the current correct decision may morph into something less desirable, or need to be reconfigured for continued and persistent success.

The Future of Our Partnership:
What Will Our Greatest Challenge Be?

- ○ Month 1_____
- ○ Month 2_____
- ○ Month 3_____
- ○ Month 4_____
- ○ Month 5_____
- ○ Month 6_____
- ○ Month 7_____
- ○ Month 8_____
- ○ Month 9_____
- ○ Month 10_____
- ○ Month 11_____
- ○ Year 1_____
- ○ Year 2_____
- ○ Year 5_____
- ○ Year 10_____
- ○ Year 15_____
- ○ Year 20_____
- ○ Year 30_____

Human Resource Management With a Twist

"If I didn't have to deal with putting out forest fires all the time, petty office politics, and squabbles, I could really get some work done and produce the things we are meant to produce!"— Countless owners, managers, employees, vendors, co-workers

Perhaps the easiest and best application of intuition in a work setting has to do with the very factors that are hardest to manage, control, predict: human behavior and relationships. These can make or break any business.

I realized at some point in my own life and work experience that these thorny issues are not the ones we have to deal with *so* we can get the work done; these issues *are* the work in any company. Whether you are making widgets, offering services, or distributing goods, it is *people* work that matters. As a leader you must understand and match personality, talent, and experience to create the proper fit. Bottom line: this is the key to any successful business operation, regardless of domain.

The more fulfilled the staff and managers are, the more productive and effective the goods and services will be produced and delivered; it is that simple. The human resources twist of gut feeling on demand can turn nightmares into dreams.

- **Assume good intent no matter how acrimonious the situation.**

Your worst workplace relationship may become one of your best in the future if you know how to understand the fundamental good intention of the other person. First, however, you have to get outside your rational mind, because your mind will play tricks on you. Reason will tell you that this person is out to get you, and tell you that there is not enough room for the two of you in this division, office, or company. *En garde!*

Using your intuition, ask yourself the question, "What is the good intention of this person who drives me nuts? How is his or her good intention actually like my own?" Don't ask a question like this when you are the most upset, mind you; wait until you have settled just a bit and are less angry or frustrated at some recent behavior or confrontation. Find the place where you meet, where you both have the best interests of the company at heart. Your intuition can help you do that. When you find that shared place, you can begin to shape your relationship around it. The knowledge itself is provided by intuition; then you turn that inner knowledge into a conscious roadmap for dealing with the difficult individual.

One of my favorite stories having to do with turning adversarial relationships into alliances comes from my time as a university academic administrator. In those years I became deeply involved in faculty labor relations and other aspects of human resource management. Most of the time I succeeded in maintaining a non-adversarial stance with faculty. After all, I was and had been full-time teaching faculty myself and loved it. I also refused to apologize for being an administrator, or to believe that integrity ended at the door of the administration building. I believe I got that part right. On another matter, though, I found myself in a real mess.

There are peculiarities to faculty employment and workload that make it difficult to rely on the usual off-the-shelf human resource information systems. Student-faculty ratios vary by academic discipline, and faculty workload includes not only classroom teaching, but also a variety of specialized courses, governance activities, scholarly research and publication, and grant-based temporary funding. Nothing out there quite met our needs in a multi-campus public university. My task was to work with someone in another office to create an information technology product that would serve one large campus in a multi-campus system.

I was getting along fine with faculty, but when tasked with developing an information system for faculty personnel matters I ran into a brick wall with the computer center. From my point of view they didn't speak English, and from their point of view I didn't speak the computer language in use at the time.

At first the relationship was quite difficult. The person in the Computer Center thought university administrators in general were uninformed, out-of-the-loop, end-users who knew nothing about technology, and she was right. We thought, in our faculty-oriented office, that technology geeks were unable to speak Standard English; could not function and provide us what we needed; and would go out of their way to avoid speaking clearly so we would look stupid. We were also right. Indeed, we were both "dead right."

In order for us to accomplish this joint task, we were required to work together, and yet working together was a task even more daunting than the end product itself. At some point the situation became so difficult that we were both called in to speak with the President of the university.

I decided unilaterally that I did not wish this relationship to be adversarial (and of course I wanted to keep my job!). Shortly after that, I began to notice that my adversary was not well respected in her own division. She had all of the requisite training and credentials; in fact, she had more than most, if not all, in her division. Suddenly, through a flash of inspiration, I realized that she was angry with us in part because she was unacknowledged in her own area and assumed the rest of us would treat her poorly too. Some of our communication difficulty had nothing to do with our department at all, but with her separate experience. She was trying to prove herself, and so was I.

But that is only part of the story, and were it not for intuition we might never have made that shift. Neither of us knew much about each other's private lives. It turns out that there were elements of our personal lives that were complicating our working relationship as well. Unexpressed concerns colored our ability to see each other and to recognize the deeper similarity. We both wanted to serve the organization in the best way we could, and we were not as far apart socially and politically as we imagined.

I was studying metaphysics formally at the time, and decided to use Jean as my subject for an intuitive exercise in class one night. The teacher asked us to choose someone we were having difficulty with, and immediately Jean popped into my mind. I did an intuitive "reading" on her from a much more detached perspective, and saw the source and meaning of the bottleneck between us. Once I "got it," my behavior towards her shifted and we remained close during the remainder of our time working together.

Jean didn't have to be in that class with me, nor did we have to go into therapy together for the shift to occur. I was willing to look deeper into both Jean's and my own concerns and good intention. I changed, and everything around me changed as well. This small example demonstrates the power of intuition in resolving "personality conflicts" in a work setting.

When I "got it" that the real issue was not entirely between us, but also affected by Jean's invisibility in her own world, I set out to make a difference in the life of this person. I was certainly visible, but in other ways needed to prove myself as well in this new job. To foster a better relationship with her, I began to acknowledge Jean publicly and privately, so that others in her division and in the university at large began to pay attention to her.

I was not the enemy, nor was she. From that moment on, we became true colleagues. Through my openness to perceive and to act on information that came in a surprising way through intuition, we reached a turning point. I continue to respect this colleague to this day, and assume the respect is mutual. Going beyond what the mind tells us permits any of us to turn adversaries into allies. I consider the turning around of that adversarial relationship, and my refusal to take an adversarial stance with faculty unions, to be among my greatest professional achievements. Conversely, I feel that the worst professional decision I ever made several years later, again having to do with technology, resulted precisely from *not* following my intuition.

Once we were able to assume good intention the work flowed easily. Sometimes the job was tedious, sometimes it involved complex discussions, and sometimes we were just exhausted trying to get the project completed. But it *was* completed with an excellent outcome. When good intention became the foundation of our working relationship, the lines of communication between us could be more direct and open. If someone asked a question or made a statement, we were able to simply hear the issue and address it. There was nothing to prove. Jointly we worked to optimize our relationship, which in turn led to optimizing the product, the service, and the organization.

Try it. Think of someone in your workplace you love to hate, the one who drives you most crazy. Ask yourself, "What is the true good intention of this person?" Write down the answer quickly, without thinking about it, in seven seconds or less. You may want to chuckle about what popped into your head! Follow that *very first* thought and see where it takes you.

Now ask yourself the question, "How is the person's good intention different from my own? Where is the place we meet? What action, if any, can I take now to reach this person through our shared good intention, even if the other individual seems unresponsive?"

Find out what a difference you can make in the fulfillment of your *own* workday, let alone the workday of someone else, by discovering the good intention of somebody else in seven seconds or less.

- **The Right Candidate for the Job**

If I told you that you could find out who the best candidate would be for a job before you hired the headhunters, before you did the background checks, before you ran reports and Myers-Briggs personality tests, would you believe me? You might be hoping against hope that this next hire would be competent, would be a good fit for the organization, would love the work, and would be committed and loyal to you. Suppose I told you that through well-developed business intuition, you could identify that person in seven seconds or less?

Keep in mind that someone who *doesn't* get the job will want to make sure you did all you could to insure that he or she was not improperly excluded from the position. With the help of intuition you can get names and initials of people *before* they apply, before you even know who the finalists will be, through applied intuition!

How is this possible? If you use blind protocols, the person giving you the intuitive information does not know in advance what you are looking for and has no investment in the outcome. If you ask a professional intuitive, for example, "Who is going to be the next hire?" which you can do even before you have any candidates at all, you might get the response, "A person with the initial JD, or two individuals, each with the initial J or D, who might be excellent candidates for this job." This is using intuition before you have any facts to back up the answer. You may not have gone to the headhunter; you may not even have a list yet of applicants for the position. However, when you start building that list and you discover that there is a candidate on that list whose initials are J or D, you pay special attention to that individual. At the very least, there may be something there worth pursuing. The person may turn out to be a surprise, may not fit the usual profile of what you would expect, but might eventually prove to be an excellent choice.

That is just one way—you might get a name or initial out of the blue. You could be wary and say, "If anybody found out I was hiring based on initials without doing my homework, I could be sued!" You are absolutely right; you could be sued. It is your responsibility to start with intuition, but then to corroborate it in some way. Find out if the information makes sense. Your gut could be wrong in this instance, depending on how confident and relaxed and detached you are about using it. Make this your starting point to help you pay attention to things that you might not ordinarily pay attention to. It is a beginning to help you love your work and your workplace.

Using Lists for Intuitive Decision Making

So what do you do? You get a list of people and ask questions. You can develop a list to find out which companies you should engage to find the hire. Imagine that you are filling a senior level position and there are several companies you have been considering as headhunters. You or someone else can write down the names of the potential headhunters first, before you get to the candidates. Assume there are three of them, for example. You write down the numbers 1-3 and you circle the number 2. Without saying anything to anybody, you just circle the number 2 because that is the one that was kind of "blinking" for you, that you felt would be the one. Then you have someone else, who does not know which number you circled, read the list of names of the potential headhunters in any order they choose.

Remember, your hunch is based on a complex configuration of energies that support your success. There are all kinds of ways to trick the rational mind; making a list and circling the number is nothing more than a "gimmick" on some level; But that intuitive device is infused with the intention to create the best outcome for you. Of all the potentialities out there, your gut feeling helps you identify the one that most suits your own development.

Using Lists For Intuitive Decision Making

○ Make a list of the candidates, options, or areas of greatest difficulty

○ Count the number of items on the list, say 3 items

○ Make a list of numbers from 1-3; just the numbers, no content

○ Without looking at the content, circle the very first number that comes to mind, for example, the number 2

○ Then go back and fill in the list, or have someone else read the list of issues, candidates, or options to you in no particular order

○ When you get to number 2, pay attention. Number 2 is the candidate or option to choose, or to be wary of, depending on how you framed the original question ("Which one to hire?" "Which one to avoid?")

So the other person reads the list and you're off and running. They name Goodrich, Lovely Right, and Terrible Choice as your companies. You circled number 2, so you start investigating Lovely Right. You say, "That's weird." But then you say, "Why not? Let's take a look at this company." Then you can ask the question, "Of the potential contact people we might work with in this company, who are the best ones for us?"

You don't stop here. What you do is *start* with the intuitive rank ordering of the list of names, and then look in the ordinary world for evidence that your intuition was on target or not. It could certainly be off target and we'll talk about that later. Intuition may be a bit better at identifying great opportunities; at the very *least* it is no worse than chance. In my experience, the thought that comes within seven seconds or less is right on the mark. And because I do this all the time, a *nanosecond* is all I really need; seven seconds seems like an eternity. Rule of thumb: the quicker the response the better.

So, locate someone who is a disinterested party and yet who is open to the intuitive process to help you identify Lovely Right (option

#2). Ask that person to investigate these three companies without knowing in advance that you have circled number 2. See what he or she finds out and what recommendations result. You can ask more than simple yes or no questions; you can frame a whole series of questions that permit you detailed information about the company. Have someone other than you corroborate or fail to corroborate the information you get intuitively.

Eventually the person tasked with the research comes back and says, "Wow, this is an interesting company!" This success will begin to increase your confidence about knowing what you know, without knowing how you know it. You will be motivated to use your gut feeling on a daily basis.

Imagine the time, energy, effort; imagine the fear, worry, concern that you can reduce by simply beginning with your gut feeling for this information. You will be amazed at how helpful this process will become.

So you have been able to find the right company to find the right person. Or you find the right resource of any kind, whether it's through a trade journal that lists individuals looking for executive level employment or a word-of-mouth network. You use all the resources that are available to you to begin to gather and cull a series of names that you might want to hire for your company. Then you make a master list: you may have 40 candidates or 100 candidates; it doesn't matter.

If the list has fewer than ten names, you can set it up quickly and write names beside the numbers. If there is a chance you might recognize any of the names, rank order the list of numbers *prior* to filling in the names of specific individuals. Without any conscious thought, you take a look at the numbers and write down the rank order for each one. For example, the fourth person on the list becomes your first choice. The third person becomes your second choice; the sixth person becomes your third choice, and so on until you now have a rank order list of the ten candidates. Now fill in the names, and these become your semi-finalists, the group that you investigate more thoroughly. Begin the rational checking, interviewing, discussing with other colleagues that you would normally do about these candidates. Once again, you will be surprised at how closely your intuitive list matches the list that is provided and ranked through customary research.

Once this occurs successfully over and over again regarding daily choices, you will learn to trust yourself more frequently and save yourself a lot of time and money on other choices of great significance to your company. Eventually you might narrow down that list to three or five candidates, and then conduct thorough interviews, invitations to your workplace, and all the things you would normally do in the interview and hiring process.

This is one way of winnowing a list that matches the best fit for your company's needs through intuition. Try it and see what happens. You still have your full list. If you don't like any of the people you selected in the first round, you can always go back into the pool. You don't have to say no to any candidate until you have tried this approach first. But if you have gone through this process several times and you discover that candidates one through ten really *are* one through ten, and that you didn't leave out anybody who should have been on the list, you begin to realize that this can work for you. As always, consult with legal counsel to make sure you commit no procedural errors and violate no institutional policy.

Once you have narrowed your field and you have a list of candidates for a position, you can start moving into greater detail with regard to each individual. You can use your intuition to answer certain questions for yourself about each candidate before you meet or know the person. You can ask intuitively, for example, "What is this person's greatest talent?" "What is this person's purpose?" "Where is this person going to be in five years?" "Why is this person interested in applying for this job?"

These are all questions that you may ask the candidate directly at a later time. Before you get on the phone or go into that room with candidates, however, ask those questions *yourself* through the source of internal guidance that is within all of us. The candidates will tell you why they are looking for a job and what they think their best gifts are; how well they work with people, places, or things; and why they think they are perfectly suited for this post. Assume good intention, and assume that your joint purpose is to make the best match for the individual and the company.

Intuitively knowing their strengths helps you; knowing their weaknesses also helps you. *Your goal is not to eliminate them; your goal is to find the best candidate for this job.* So ask those questions—you are not prying—get the answers, and then use the answers you get to assist you at every phase of the recruitment process. Keep your gut feeling active when you interview the potential candidates, when you do background checks on them, and when you talk with others who serve as references for them. This is a tool that can save you time, money, and lots of heartache if you use it appropriately.

Once you are in a room with an individual, other observational techniques can kick in as well, such as those described in *Blink*. When you are speaking with a candidate who is telling his or her personal story, intuition is always working for you, whether or not you are paying active attention. Wherever you are, whether in a conference room or on the phone, someone is telling you her version of her story. You will begin to notice impulses or feelings, or something that says, "This person is right on the mark." or "I just don't feel that this person is telling me the truth." You can rely on your gut not only to identify the individual, but also to assess what you are hearing from other relevant individuals as you go through the interview process.

Your body may talk to you; you may have hunches or feelings; you may have subtle sensations that say, "Uh, oh. Something's wrong here." Conversely, you might feel the excitement that "Something's *right* here!"

Once you know you like Candidate #2, you might ask yourself intuitive questions like, "Is this person going to like us? What actions do we need to take in order to provide an environment in which this candidate can blossom?" "What action, if any, can we take to ensure the best possible fit between the new hire and the rest of us who are already here? What can we do to accommodate this transition?"

Remember that you are walking a two-way street: not only do you want this candidate to be an excellent fit for the company, but the company has got to be an excellent fit for the potential hire as well. Otherwise, there is no mutual fulfillment and problems arise. Asking, "What can we do for this person?" is not only good personnel practice, it is a way to go deeper and know what makes the person shimmer. That's how it works, and that's how you do it. That's what creates mutual satisfaction with the process.

- **The Right Job**

So you know you hired the right person. Now there are a bunch of other things to do to make sure this relationship works. Is this right person in the right job, department, or office? The individual gets along great with you, but you will not be the immediate boss; conversely, he or she will be supervising others, reporting only to you.

Frame intuitive questions to determine if this is the right supervisor in the right division at the right time. Sometimes this is the right employee, but you need to wait six months to bring the individual on board because other structural changes will occur during the interim that might affect his or her placement. See if both location and supervision are right. You are bringing in someone to diversify the business: is this the right one to diversify, or just the right one to be part of your team? These are all questions you can ask and answer, beginning to receive the answer in seven seconds or less.

If what you get corroborates the choices you have made, then proceed, negotiate, and talk with others. Continue to do all the things in a regular business day the way you would normally do, simply adding this additional resource and support. You have your internal cheerleading squad that says "Rah! Rah! Go do it!" Alternatively, "This is not right . . . wait; check this out first, confirm, rearrange your options."

This is how you blend intuitive information that comes from that inspired gut feeling with daily business practice. By the time you do all the things you are supposed to do, the way any good employer would do, your gut feeling has not gotten you in trouble or made you vulnerable to litigation. It has simply helped you streamline your process. In turn the candidate comes online more quickly, hits the ground running, and is supported by others in the company. If the person is not going to be supported by others, your intuition will give you a heads up. "This is a great person, great fit, great timing. This is someone who should definitely be in my company, but I have another employee who is going to be really upset when I've hired this person. How do I handle that? I know I want to hire candidate #2 even though I know the decision will generate tension."

Go back and find the good intention that has put the current employee in resistance mode. "Why will this employee be upset if we bring in the new candidate? Is there some way to reshape the current employee's authority, role, or function that will lessen the frustration and make him or her less concerned with what the new person is doing?" All of this requires simple utilization of an idea that hits the corners of the mind before you have time to complicate things unnecessarily. "What have I failed to notice because I have not invested the same kind of effort into the current employee that I put into this new hire? After all, I am expecting the new hire to turn the company around and clean up the mess."

Avoiding Grievances

In the mid-1980s I was an academic administrator responsible for faculty labor relations. To help prepare me for this role I attended training conducted by a management-oriented company. The training brochure emphasized management practices to avoid unionization. There was considerable national debate at the time about the relative value of decertifying existing unions or avoiding the creation of new ones.

Most colleagues in attendance came clearly as management representatives, and probably assumed they would find an oasis where they would be told all sorts of terrible things about "them," the others, the difficult employees. What actually happened came as a surprise to many: we spent a week learning how to *recognize and acknowledge* employees! Union avoidance really meant management awareness. Grievance avoidance meant knowing how to recognize in advance when an employee was disgruntled or unhappy; when there was inappropriate fit; when there was someone who had been working hard but not acknowledged; when it was time to make a change, to promote; when, as a last resort, if there were no fit, to end the employment of that individual.

There is no greater tool for avoiding grievances in the workplace than well-honed intuition.

Where there is an assumption of good intention, there is less need to go down an adversarial path. Managers have a heads up that something is wrong long before the situation reaches crisis proportion. The need for progressive discipline or termination declines significantly. Management and union maintain an open and trustworthy line of communication.

How many individuals in your workplace need acknowledgment? How many senior managers and *bosses* in your workplace need acknowledgment? All of us have bosses, even if the boss is the Board of Directors or the head of a parent company. If you are a boss, you need acknowledgment. Getting acknowledged by others helps you recognize and give it to others. How many of us take the time to acknowledge another's talent and performance? How many of have had someone else acknowledge ours?

In seven seconds or less find out how your employees and managers are doing. Find out what the best form of acknowledgment is for them that can keep them happy and productive. Do you want to know if you need to send a card or flowers, or to say something or not say something? Frame the question and take the first answer you get in seven seconds or less; then act on the answer you receive. The very first thought or impulse is usually the correct one. Acknowledge first, acknowledge regularly, acknowledge up and down and sideways in the hierarchy. Let people know that you see them, not that you are prying. You want to let them know that you are interested in their development, their work, and their performance. The *One Minute Manager*[12] is terrific; the seven seconds manager gives an added bonus.

You might start your day with a few simple questions: "Where shall I go today? Which employee needs my attention?" "Which question should I tackle?" You may get a name, a division, some clue or phrase: "Check out the advertising division or the health care area." Follow that hunch to see what happens.

Be proactive and avoid grievances whenever possible. Be aware. Pay attention. Be defenseless in framing questions. Then when you receive an impulse, an answer, a phrase, a symbol, find out what the clue means and act on it.

Be grounded in the basics of employee relations and human resource management. When someone comes to you with a presenting problem or issue, you don't have to be a psychologist or psychiatrist to know how to assess the information presented. When someone says to you, "I'm really upset about the way so and so is treating me in a particular office or division," you can ask the interior question, "What is the true concern of this employee? What is the fear lurking behind this personality dispute? What is the structural issue that is not being addressed?" Personality conflicts in the workplace almost always have to do with structural issues. Use your intuition to ask:

- "In this situation, what structural issues can I address that would improve this work situation?"
- "Would these two parties still be angry at each other if they had more clarity about their responsibilities and roles?"
- "Is one of these individuals reporting to two different people with two conflicting sets of values and priorities?"
- "Is this individual having to do the work of three people instead of one?"

- "Are there impacts on the work of this individual that stem from a missed or unstated connection in a different part of the organization?'

You do not have to excuse yourself from the room and go meditate in a closet. You can take a deep breath, listen fully, and then pay attention to the clues that will begin immediately to form in your mind. This is another way in which you, as a manager, can avoid grievances. And you can do this in a flash as you sit around the conference table.

Of course there are difficult employees and situations; of course there are attempts to bring resolution, none of which satisfy a particular person or party. But most often when that occurs the bitterness has built incrementally over years and sometimes decades without action, notice, or acknowledgment. See the future impact of current and past personnel decisions. See the impact of failing to utilize the true talents of your employees before things get so bad that you are required to engage in drastic measures. Intuition is your best HR Director. Using it in conjunction with qualified, experienced, compassionate executives means you won't have to worry about troublesome employees and grievances, or the formation of those "terrible unions." You will be aware far in advance of any of those eventualities. If your company is already unionized, use these techniques to determine the good intention of union members, and work with those in the union who share your desire for success.

When you reach a moment and know that a change must occur, you can use intuitive information to know when, whether, and how to make necessary changes. This includes decisions such as whether or not to continue with particular divisions and employees, and whether or not it would be best to transfer individuals from one area of the company to another.

For example, if you are considering transferring someone within the company, make a list of the people with whom this employee will be working following the transfer. You can frame a question simply: "Will the fit work?"

Given the list of prospective co-workers in the new situation, identify the one who is going to be most at ease with the transition and the one who will offer the greatest resistance to it. Take the information you receive from your now trusted gut feeling and have conversations as needed and appropriate with people in the receiving department. What is their good intention? What are their fears? What do they know that you have failed to notice? Most importantly, don't just drop somebody on a unit without consulting with the affected individuals in advance.

Most often when transfers occur, they occur because one area wants to get rid of somebody who is problematic, or an employee wants to get away from somebody problematic. The old department head has no interest in whether or not the receiving department is willing, interested, or able to integrate this person into the new environment; he or she just wants the problem gone. Ask questions and find out, for example, "What will be the biggest sticking point or best match?" Determine what action, if any, would be appropriate to ease this transition, particularly if the person being transferred is coming in as a supervisor of people who have been there for a long time.

These are such simple things, and yet frequently we do not take time to vocalize these dilemmas, or to discuss the situation in depth with anyone.

You will still be required to be tactful with interested parties. It is unlikely you would say to someone who is being transferred, or to the unit receiving this person, "Oh, by the way, I have this hunch that you are going to have a hard time with Chandra or Joe's transfer to this area." Use intuitive information instead to frame the conversation in your own mind, then sit down and have a conversation with the individuals or group and ask in standard business language, "How are you feeling about the new person joining your team? How are you feeling about changes that might impact your job description?"

"What kinds of things can we work on to make sure *you* are satisfied and happy with these new events and structures? Let's talk . . . what are you most concerned about?" When you listen (if they are willing to speak), be defenseless in the listening and use that inner voice or guidance to say, "Yes, this is exactly right." You might also find yourself saying, "Hmmm, I hadn't thought of that implication." Alternatively, you might feel the employee or team member is not being honest and direct. If you feel the individual is not being open, ask another question and seek clarification. Push further until you feel you are getting authentic feedback.

Intuition helps you know whom to hire, fire, or transfer, and whose job responsibilities to redesign or reassign. Furthermore, it helps you get the work done with well-matched, productive employees. It saves you time, money, heartache, unwanted surprise, work lost handling grievances, work lost dealing with employee uprisings because employees feel they are not being heard. Best of all, there is *no* financial cost associated with using this tool. Your gut feeling is the best set of ears you could ever hope to have for your successful business.

As you see success after success and begin to truly trust those hunches, your workplace will improve dramatically. Furthermore, as you foster the use and acceptance of intuition throughout the organization at every level, everyone will notice the difference, even if they cannot figure out exactly what is different and why. Since such a large proportion of your life is spent working, make it good work!

With the added factor of intuition, maintaining appropriate boundaries becomes more important than ever. The romantic comedy called "What Women Want" comes to mind. In the film, Mel Gibson's character accidentally gains access to women's thoughts, and is faced with a series of ethical dilemmas. He works for an advertising firm and uses his intuitive ability to steal other people's ideas and claim them as his own. He also learns a lot about women's private thoughts about men, and then uses this knowledge in order to increase his popularity and be seen as a sensitive male. Because Gibson was an interested party and workplace competitor, he misused what was portrayed as a special and accidental gift, and eventually learned the hard way to honor other people's boundaries, especially those of Helen Hunt, who played his romantic lead. While "What Women Want" was a fanciful romantic comedy, CEO's, managers, and co-workers face such issues on a daily basis. Questions of privacy, workplace romance, intellectual property, organizational succession planning and restructuring, and maintaining a competitive edge constantly test your ethical resolve and the resolve of everyone around you.

Here are some common sense tips to keep you on the straight and narrow.

Tips for Ethical Practice, Especially When Using Intuition

○ Establish and maintain clear interpersonal boundaries: say what you mean, mean what you say, and avoid dissembling or outright lying to get information from people that you plan to use against them

○ Limit exchanges and reporting of personal information: use the water cooler and executive washroom to further company success, but not at the expense of a colleague

○ Master the proper communication and use of sensitive information. Some things you have a bona fide need to know and to communicate appropriately. Be discerning and decipher what is truly relevant and important

○ Avoid actual and potential conflicts of interest

○ Recognize and manage organizational politics

○ Recognize and manage sexual harassment, innuendos, and *quid pro quo* expectations. Many labor relations books and workshops address the thorny issue of personal boundaries. For our purposes here, use your intuition to help you know how to act or refrain from acting in any given situation.

○ Remember, discernment is key

Trust

"How can I trust myself if I do not trust human nature in general?"
"How can I trust myself if I do not trust anybody else in particular?"

There is *always* someone trustworthy in an organization. You just have to figure out who it is, and then trust that individual or group. It is easy to think that you are the only one who cares, or is competent, or can keep a confidence. The old saying, "If you want anything done you'd better do it yourself!" is repeated as often today as when it was first uttered. The truth of the matter is, there will *always* be good company around you when you slow down long enough to find, nourish, and develop it.

Recently a colleague did an intuitive session for me. I am so used to using intuition for everybody else, sometimes I forget to use it for myself! Furthermore, I do not know too many people who do it as well as I like to think I do. In the course of our conversation the colleague looked directly at me with a look that was warm, and also a tad impatient. "Helen, you are not the only one, you know. You have company in the world."

That was an important moment for me. I didn't have to carry the weight of the "authentically intuitive" label on my shoulders, singlehandedly countering beliefs that people who engage in this work are flighty or charlatans. I also didn't have to carry the martyrdom and not-so-thinly veiled arrogance and narcissism that proclaimed, "Nobody is as good as I am at this." I have reminded myself frequently following that conversation that I am not the only one, and in doing so others have stepped forward to help. I can trust myself and I can trust human nature.

No organization, including a sole proprietorship, can exist without trusting somebody else. Find those in your organization whom you can trust and trust them. Like Robert's CEO colleagues, they wish you well and they will help you realize your vision for your company when you give them a chance.

Good Intention, Even When We Drive Each Other Crazy

Think of one person in your work life who drives you absolutely nuts. Take the very first name that pops into your head, even if that name is a surprise to you. You may have thought rationally that dealing with somebody else was harder, but if a different name from the one you might have expected pops up, go with it

Then ask yourself the question, "What is the good intention _____ is trying to express by this crazy-making behavior? There must be some good intention regarding our shared work together, or _____ wouldn't be so stubborn and difficult!" Don't think about this . . . just scribble something down *fast*. What is he or she caring about so deeply that it is making both of you frustrated and emotionally taxed? And remember always, *always* take the very first thought that comes to mind in seven seconds or less . . . a nanosecond is even better!

Now ask yourself in the same way, very quickly: "What action on my part, if any, could improve the situation between me and _____?" Remember, it is entirely possible that no action is required or even useful; there may be nothing to do. Was there ever a time when you did get along? If so, what went sour? All you need is a word or phrase, i.e., "She betrayed me." or, "He'll step on anybody to get ahead."

For just a moment now, suspend disbelief and imagine one thing you could do or say unilaterally, regardless of what the other person understands or does not understand, does or does not do. What would that one thing be? Are you willing to do it, even if you have absolutely no expectation your action would "work" or improve the situation?

Here is a last important area for questions that ultimately lead to understanding fundamental good intention. Answer all without a thought. Long hand is better than typing for this exercise.

- "How am I like _____?" (I'm sure you have thought often and long about how you are different! Look at the other side for a change.)

- "What is it in me that triggers this intense reaction to this colleague? Who in my family acts like that?" (I'll bet somebody does!)
- "What is my good intention in being so upset with him/her? What do I care about so deeply that is threatened by _____'s off-the-wall behavior? Clarity perhaps, or ease, or control, or a positive image, or a calm environment, or financial success? Is anything *actually* threatened, or is it just my fear that something could be threatened, like my sanity? Maybe _____ will throw a monkey wrench into the usual way of doing things, or really hurt the bottom line."
- "Is there another way to handle this that diffuses the situation?"

Remember, there may be absolutely nothing to do. But if you find appropriate actions to take by asking and answering these questions so quickly that you bypass the rational part of your brain, *do them* and see what happens!!

Lastly, detach from the outcome. Have fun with it and wait to be surprised. Maybe now someone will give a war and you won't have to attend!

Enhancing Collaborative Relationships
"What Is The Presenting Issue?"

_____

_____

_____

_____

_____

> ## "What One Action, If Any, Is Appropriate For Resolution?"
>
> _____
>
> _____
>
> _____
>
> _____
>
> _____
>
> _____
>
> _____

Sometimes it's not about you. Sometimes it's not even about the company. Often the presenting issue is not the most important thing to consider. Intuition helps you look beneath the surface of presenting issues and workplace conflict to find out what is _really_ going on. Someone could be sick, or in the middle of a messy divorce, or caring for aging parents or delinquent children. Someone could be losing a home. As I recall, the rule of thumb in human resource literature is that the employee is out of whack for at least a year when there is a divorce, birth, death, or purchase of a home. There may also be medical problems, substance abuse, and even mental illness. All of these factors affect performance, yet they are not always the _result_ of employment issues. Let's return to the case of Jean in the Computer Center.

Each of our units had some pretty harsh words for the other. But, catching my breath and tucking my ego aside for a moment, I realized that some of this had nothing to do with me. On the other hand, some of it absolutely did. Both of us were in difficult roles in our respective units. I knew nothing about information systems, and yet here I was in charge of creating one in collaboration with all those techies, who probably considered us impossible to teach.

The light went on in my head, and I realized that we had to find a place to meet in the middle: Jean would learn to communicate with us non-technical folks in Standard English, and I would learn COBOL and how to design data element dictionaries. I took some courses and fell in love with information technology. Suddenly I understood what the word "just" meant when we were asking them to "just" do something that required programming for us in COBOL. These were the old days when you had to go through and find every instance where something occurred and make a zillion programming changes for one minor "just," or one more "We've changed our minds and want to add another field to the database."

We began to meet in the middle and to speak the same language. We became an interdivisional team and did a bang up job on that faculty database. In fact we did such a good job that other campuses in our multi-campus system adopted it as well.

Based in part on my training as a sociologist, I believe that what appear to be personality conflicts in the workplace almost always have structural problems at the core. Framing good intuitive questions can help elicit what those unrecognized structural issues might be, such as confused or dual reporting relationships, confusing job descriptions, looming layoffs, and many other factors.

Intuitive Human Resource Management
In Seven Seconds Or Less

o   Assume good intent and find it no matter how acrimonious the situation

o   Assume middle ground exists and find it

o   Address fear on the part of any party

o   Ask intuitively for the best outcome, structure, or decision that fulfills both individual and company: take the very first answer that begins to form in seven seconds or less

o   Ask what action, *if any*, would be appropriate to change or improve the situation or relationship

o   Is the relationship too far gone to rehabilitate? Know when to give up on it

o   Ask if the intent or action of *indirect* parties to your relationship (or the relationship between parties you manage) is affecting the outcome of this situation

o   Using gut feeling first, discover the impact of current or future *policies* on *people* in the company

o   Ask if there are any policies or procedures to rethink; then follow up on the answer

o   Consider that structured and expected adversarial relationships, such as those between management and labor, need not be so adversarial: each needs the company; each needs the other. Look for surprises using intuitive tools

o   Discern the real or deeper issue from the presenting one

o   Determine appropriate forms of acknowledgment for employees: know what matters to them

o   Determine the best time for you or someone else to leave the company; and the best time to diversify the business or workforce

Trying Time

The thorniest problem of all with intuitive decision making is getting the timing right. Good information but bad timing makes a mess. Conversely, good timing but bad or incomplete information can have the same result.

I recall working with a client on a personal matter: he was wondering about the possibility of a new relationship. I told him that he would meet someone within 30 days with a particular set of initials, and that this relationship would be fantastic. He contacted me later and told me that he had indeed met this person, who happened to have the very initials I had given him, and that their life together was fantastic. We were both very pleased that I had been able to help him, even though he did not typically trust such information.

I heard nothing from the client for several years, but had occasion to contact him later. He said, "Helen, you were right about my finding this love in 30 days, and you got everything right, except that she is *nuts!*" Apparently she became obsessed with him and made his life miserable, in essence loving him *too* much. By the time we got in touch again, he had left her and moved out of state, partly to get away from her. Timing is clearly only *part* of the equation.

From the perspective of intuition, past, present, and future are equidistant in terms of our capacity to retrieve information. All probabilities stem from and are shaped by this particular moment in time. Current perception always rules, or what some call the "moment point."[13]

There are many intuitives who dare not venture into the future, for fear of being wrong, fear of taking power away from clients, or fear of the unknown. I have a different perspective on this issue and jump into making statements about past, present, and future with both feet. Businesses need as much information about the future as they can scrounge up, which is why businesses, more than any other sector except perhaps the military, are willing to hire intuitives and futurists, while others avoid us like the plague.

Venturing across time helps you decide whether what is most likely to occur in the future is what you really *wish* to happen. You can get an immediate response, such as:

"Yes, let's go there!"

Or "Yes, with conditions."

Or "No, that doesn't look good. We need to re-evaluate and make different choices."

Time, especially time with the benefit of intuition, is a friend. It is neither feared adversary nor superstitious bogeyman. No one can take away someone else's authority to decide which actions to take. Rather, what I am continually told as evidence for intuition is, "You helped me frame what I already knew to be the appropriate action in my own heart and mind."

For an organized approach to applied intuition and time, separating the *number* or data point from the *unit* of time is a big help. The number comes quickly; the unit of time often involves more interference from the rational mind. For example, it is quite easy for the number seven to pop into your mind when somebody asks you to just make up a number, or to pick a number between one and ten. However if I ask you to tell me whether the seven is related to days, weeks, months, or years, you might start to get a little shaky, wondering, "What is she up to?" Suddenly the rational mind takes over.

The best way to succeed with timing issues is to trick the rational mind by parsing the question: get the number itself first, then go for the unit of time. Numbers can pop into the mind effortlessly, probably because they don't make much sense and it seems like you are just "making it up." You are indeed, but the making up is not by chance.

Units of time, however, are a bit trickier. If you get that something big is going to happen in a few days when that seems rationally improbable and even impossible, reason kicks in very quickly to make it difficult for you to choose a unit of time that comes soon. On the other hand, if you choose a unit of time that is far out when you are anxiously awaiting a quick reply, your rational mind will once again jump into denial mode and look for something sooner.

That is why visualizing the unit of time like a spinning roulette wheel helps you "land" on the appropriate answer: days, weeks, months, years. Or you could just repeat the units in your mind and pick the one that feels strongest. Of course it is possible to add smaller units of time to the chart, especially if you are a day trader when hours and nanoseconds make a difference. But for most ordinary business decisions, beginning with days works just fine. You can also get the number first, and then decide the decimal places or zeros afterwards. This is especially useful when looking at issues like selling or buying prices and interest rates. Get the non-zero numbers first, and then figure out where they go. Is it 46 or 46,000 or 4.6 million? I can know, for example, that there is something having to do with the numbers 4 and 6, and the client will understand how many zeros or decimal places are relevant.

This is an exercise you can do alone, or once again you can ask a buddy to give you the numbers without disclosing the topic. With intuition, especially when you are emotionally attached to the outcome, knowing less is often better when you are about to make a heart thumping decision!

Intuitive Timing Tips

Potential Event	Num	D	W	M	Y	Crisis #	Opp#
Bad news	17		√			5-15D	10W
Launch	2				√	3.5Y	17Y
CEO chg.	5			√		2Y	6W

1. Get the number FIRST without thinking.
2. Then imagine a roulette wheel spinning: days, weeks, months, years? See which unit of time is most likely and check that box.
3. Ask, "When will a problem arise with this product or process?" Repeat figuring out the time frame and fill in the Crisis# with a unit of time next to it.
4. Ask, "When will the optimum moment arise to diversify, modify, or improve this element or product, or to avoid an impending problem or surprise?" Fill in the Opportunity# and a unit of time next to it.

Perhaps had we taken the time to look at that personal client's relationship with his new girlfriend farther out than their finding each other in 30 days, I might have been able to help him avoid the pitfall of being loved nearly to death some time later!

There are at least seven different types of time horizons to consider intuitively when it comes to business cycles and time: initial event horizon, peak implementation or plateau period, challenge of crisis or loss, challenge of opportunity or growth, blindside event or surprise, diversification ahead of decline, and succession planning. Hitting these timing points well is high art for both quantitative and intuitive methodologies, and key to a positive bottom line. The chart above helps identify those moments in the future when you and the company will need to pay particular attention to avoid pitfalls and to embrace opportunities for further success. More detail will follow, of course, to flesh out the precise nature of these moments, but it is highly beneficial to have some inkling well in advance as to the most likely timeframe for paying attention.

Any of these event horizons can be anticipated or unanticipated, and each carries its own intensity. Business literature is full of tales about the challenges of growth and expansion, not just of contraction and loss. Getting a handle on timeframe for these events aids enormously in strategic planning for the future. While improbable, Nassim Taleb's "Black Swan" events[14] are not necessarily or completely *unknown* possibilities; it is the *timing* of these possibilities that creates the greatest havoc for markets and societies. Market corrections occur, earthquakes, fires and floods ravage the land, and political parties win and lose unexpectedly. Even assassinations are not out of the realm of expectation. In fact none of these dramatic possibilities is an unfamiliar occurrence, no matter how devastating; but the inability to plan ahead and to pinpoint the *timing* of the events shakes confidence to the core. Scenario planning and the academic discipline of futures studies attempt to capture and quantify these potentialities, along with estimating long-term outcomes and costs.[15] The goal of scenario planning is always predictability and control, yet these methodologies usually shun intuitive approaches that assist predictability, precisely because such methodologies are not rational. Surprise is *never* rational, and as Carl Jung said, intuition is "not contrary to reason; it is outside the domain of reason."

With the help of intuition it is possible to actually *go* to various futures and see what is most likely to occur, given what is happening now personally and professionally. It is possible to view business entities in this way, as well as individuals and groups.

Traveling Through Time

There is general consensus that in the dream state time does not matter. In the intuitive state time does not matter either. The rule of thumb for me is, "If it can be imagined, it already exists in the field of probabilities." Intuition helps visit that field without having to book an airline ticket; it helps travel inwardly. In that interior domain reason and apparent nonsense work closely together, blending variables that would be ignored if one were using the rational mind and quantitative analysis alone.

It is possible to actually visit the person you will most likely be in the future, the one who is most fulfilled, and to ask that "probable" you what it took to get there, to be so radiant in your future personal and professional life.[16] By probable you I mean the aspect of yourself that will be expressed optimally in the future if you follow your gut feeling now. It is also possible to see what the company will look like in its most successful future moment. Here's a device to help you connect with your future individual self. You can also use the exercise to connect with the future of your business. I recommend that initially you do the exercise in an *open-ended manner first*, and then perhaps use it again later to visit a particular time frame, such as five or ten years ahead.

> *Imagine you are standing on a hill, perhaps at dusk, and you look over and see the lights of a town or village off in the distance. See yourself walking (or driving or flying!) towards the inviting lights of that place in the future. When you get there, look around. What kind of place is this? Look at the locale, look at the people, if any. Where is it? What is going on generally?*
>
> *Now look around until you find yourself in a scene there. Think of this future version of yourself in the third person for the time being: what is he or she doing? If this is a company, what is going on in the company, and what is that person's role in it? What is happening that makes the individual shimmer with delight and radiate that delight outwards?*

In this space outside of time, you can actually talk to this future version of yourself and ask what he or she is doing and why. More importantly, you can ask what happened in the past to create this present satisfaction. Not only can you ask; you can also get answers! From the perspective of this future self, your questions are easy to answer because your present dilemma is now a part of its past. In the future the problem has already been resolved in one way or the other. The response will be something like, "Oh, that's easy, I just . . ."

Because your present is your future self's past, things are so much easier to observe. They are detached from the emotion of the present crisis, so you can take advantage of that future perspective to help you make decisions _now_.

If the scenario is desirable, you can know with compassion and detachment that a particular option you are considering in the present works the way you might have intended. You can also see multiple probabilities and futures in one sweeping look. This look need not be literally visual, although it could be, but the sense of contentment is unmistakable, and the circumstances of that contentment come pouring into your awareness.

When the moment shifts—say you look at next week instead of today, or next year—that future self will adapt to your changed circumstances and interim decisions in the twinkling of an eye. It will adjust and show you the best possible future self from that new place. Your conversation can be as general or detailed as you wish.

One nice device when you visit the future this way is to mentally ask your future self for a gift, usually something small that can fit in the palm of your hand. Look at the gift in your mind's eye, and hold it in your mental hand. At some moment in your "real" future, the one that occurs inside of time, you will come across that object. When this happens, you will recognize the object immediately, a real-time indication that you are indeed on the best path towards the optimal outcome you saw in your mental journey. If you already have such an object in your possession, then this is a clue that you are indeed on track to your desired goals.

This exercise is literally playing with time, and with the help of intuition you learn to play in the field of probabilities with concrete success. This process is somewhat tricky to describe in words, but quite easy to do, and great fun to experience. *Bon voyage!*

Simple Choices

One of my favorite pastimes is playing intuition telephone with a group of friends. One of us will pick up the phone and say,

"Pick a number between 1 and 5."

"Two and a half."

"Two and a *half*??

"Yes. Closest to two, but there seems to be something else not on your list, maybe a combination of option two and one of the others you wrote down." Or the response might be:

"Two. Definitely two."

"Ok, thanks. Bye!" [click]

Usually we will just laugh out loud, not explaining what in the world we were talking about, and go on about our daily routine. The subject may or may not come up later, and we just move on. At other times we end up having a long subsequent discussion about the matter and how the friend's intuitive response was right on the mark. Sometimes the question *was* incomplete and other combinations were found to be more desirable. Sometimes the answer was simple and straightforward. It is amazing how accurate and useful that trick can be when you are all willing to play along with the intuitive mind. If someone gives you a call like that, take the very first response that pops into your head, and let it go the way we do when we say, "Ok, thanks. Bye!"

These friends are not all just calling me, as the "professional" intuitive. Any of us will call on any of the others just as quickly. Intuition doesn't just belong to the professional; it is the birthright of everyone! Ultimately, there is no mystery behind the veil.

In no way do I mean to imply, however, that all questions can be resolved this quickly or easily. There are complex situations that may require a more multifaceted approach. Begin here, though: if an issue seems to be complex, see if you can break it down into a series of simple choices, whether yes-no-maybe options, or 1-2-3 options. You might even take the thorny issue of timeline options and frame it this way in order to take the investment of emotional energy out of the intuitive process and decision making. For example, option 1 could be six months, option 2 twelve months, and option 3 eighteen months. The friend's answer to your list could be something like, "I got none of the above." Or, not knowing the question had to do with time, "Much more." Your friend may have not known whether the options you were asking about had to do with a price, a candidate, a timeline, or which restaurant you should choose for dinner! And for the friend it doesn't matter, since he or she is completely detached from the outcome.

If, on the other hand, I were to ask my friend to pick a number between one and three, and let slip I was considering a multimillion dollar investment, that would be enough to keep this buddy from being willing to risk an answer. The rational mind would take over with, "I'd better stay out of that one! I don't want to be responsible for making a mistake and having my friend lose so much money." The intuitive process is exactly the same for choosing a restaurant for dinner as for choosing an investment option, but the long-term consequences would be quite different. That is precisely why blind and sometimes double-blind questions are preferred: they help provide detachment from the outcome, and they get out of the way so true intuition can kick in.

Putting it All Together: Sound Potential for New Product Development

An unusual man entered my life unexpectedly in 2002.

Recently retired to Florida, Kevin felt that his life's work wasn't done. He suggested that we partner up to build a new company from scratch, based upon intuitive design. His proposal sounded like fun, and it seemed as if our skills complemented each other beautifully, so I said, "Let's go for it!"

One of the first things we did was to take an organized look at the state of sound technology, triggered in part by an exercise we created called "25 Intuited Ideas for a Changing World."

After sixty to eighty hours of intuitive questions and answers about sound, we felt we were poised to make a difference. (Remember, the answers in each instance would begin to come in seven seconds or less.) We could be guinea pigs in embedding intuition in an open way at every level of an organization. Another colleague and sound expert from New York also helped us in the early stages, as well as Kevin's life partner Sylvia. We imagined that we would become the company to design tools that would help scientists make *future* generations of tools. In this way, scientists would be able to delve even deeper into the wondrous workings of nature.

Sure enough, after some focused research on trends in existing larger companies, there seemed to be promising opportunities in the area of nanotechnology and sound. We also developed a blueprint for an entertainment product to introduce our new sound technology to a broader public market.

Kevin became ill and died about 18 months after we began this project, so we never found out how far we could go. What follows, however, are tips we learned at the very earliest stages about the use of intuition in the development of a new product, service, and organization.

- **Start with intuition: begin with a sudden spurt of inspiration, a waking dream, a feeling, an image, a trigger in your environment that piques your interest.**
  The very first event was an inspired thought or hunch that seemed to come from nowhere. I had been reading an August 2002 Business Week article on "25 Ideas for a Changing World" with interest, and mentioned it to colleagues in our regular meetings. Suddenly the thought hit: "Why don't we propose 25 *intuited* ideas for a changing world?" I no longer remember who started it, but that simple question began what eventually became a source of impassioned inquiry, even leading to the formation of a company to design a multi-sensory product made of various specific materials. I was always interested in the intuitive side of things, but Kevin was keen to start a company. I went along with him on this, but felt increasingly uncomfortable; it was *impossible* to be a disinterested party. In hindsight and after losing Kevin to illness, I am more convinced than ever that the best intuition comes from the ability to remain detached from the outcome. That is why you sometimes need third party input when applying intuition to issues with strong emotional meaning for you.

As a subscriber to *Business Week*, I may have kicked off the discussion based on that article, while my colleagues Edward and Kevin, who were aware of our desire to speak to the mainstream, probably suggested the word "intuited" for a what might otherwise have been considered a more esoteric term. Lincoln, another colleague and mentor, showed me an article entitled the "Art of the Brilliant Hunch" in *Business 2.0*[17].

Before we knew it the tape recorder was rolling and we were scurrying off into the realm of sound. Below are unedited excerpts from our actual meetings and conversations in 2002 and 2003. More than anything else, they show in detail how our process worked.

> Edward: . . . outline what new businesses will have to think about.
>
> Helen: The first thing has to do with hearing, because it is an apt metaphor for all that is occurring in the world at this time. Innovation in sound will affect every technology currently utilized anywhere.
>
> Edward: You were talking about the relationship between sound and intention . . .
>
> Helen: Very shortly intention will be measurable by sound, by frequency. Just as people use EEG's, EKG's, and all of these other medical devices; lie detectors to measure truth or lies . . . sound in its subtleties will provide a deeper knowing of humanity than any other sense that has been explored to date. This will mean that music will change, listening and recording devices will change. There will be abuses of this knowledge, as well as enhancements. Marketing will become sound focused. Advertising will become sound focused. Healing will become sound focused. And instrumentation for alignment of the physical body, and perhaps for organizations not too long afterwards, will be sound focused. This is "muzak" taken to a very different level.

- **Step Two: Using the intuited information, begin to conduct appropriate research by reading, talking with experts in the field, searching the Web. Use intuitive methods to winnow the list of potential sources, backers, scholars, experts, competitors, and locations.**

If the information provides clues to future developments that currently do not exist, it is important to find out what is typically called the current "state of the art" in your particular field of inquiry or manufacturing or service.

In the university, graduate students sometimes resist the requirement to link the subject of their doctoral dissertation to historical and intellectual traditions of their field. They want to feel they are "reinventing the wheel." They may also want to ignore the possibility that so-called less developed individuals or societies may have thought a very long time ago about what they consider now to be new.

Businesses, on the other hand, cannot afford to waste time or money, so they spend a great deal of time and money up front trying to limit what they are required to make "from scratch." It would be beneficial to use existing devices in new ways or at a fraction of the cost to produce entirely new components.

As a business leader, it is important to talk with colleagues you trust, remembering that there are only a few degrees of separation between you and any resource you might need to complete your prototype or to bring your ostensibly new product to market. Even if you do not know who these potential resources might be, you can use a combination of intuition and plain old database surfing to find out who might be of direct assistance, or who could point you to one who might be the critical resource you need.

A client of mine had finally secured a patent for her product's conceptual design and was ready to move ahead to develop the prototype. Through a series of well-framed questions during an intuitive session, she discovered that there were individuals in her immediate geographical vicinity who might help in this next important phase of her work. Several of these individuals she already knew or knew about, so access to them would be easy and much less costly than traveling all over the country looking for experts. All she needed was right there in her own back yard, and this discovery came about through intuitive means!

In our fledgling sound-oriented company we developed what we called our "List of 100." The list included people, companies, related products, and researchers on the subject of sound . . . everything we had been able to track down to date from our individual and collective research. In many cases I didn't know who the people were, or why they were on our list; my colleagues did most of that searching. This created an opportunity to let intuition order the list and help us set immediate, near-term, and long-term priorities.

We needed to get the list down from 100 to first, second, and third tier contacts. So we simply typed up the list in no particular order, perhaps the order of discovery, adding as we went along. In our regular session (always taped on both sides of the telephone), we identified quite quickly the first five people or companies to contact. Having never laid eyes on the list my partners had prepared, I gave them five numbers: 17, 48, 55, 3, and 21. Then we went to the list and circled the number selected through the intuitive "reading."

The results were nothing short of astounding: not only did the selection of the five as first tier contacts make perfect sense, but two of the five were actually the same individual, with the name spelled differently. That individual is one of the world's foremost researchers in sound and a perfect source to introduce our work and find out if we truly were on to something important, or were simply "tuning in" intuitively to already existing concepts and products.

As we went through the short list selected using intuitive means, I began to ask, "Who is that person?" "What is that company?" My other colleagues Sylvia and Kevin had been going through old sessions, doing research on the web, finding bits and pieces of paper with names scribbled for future reference, and finally put together for my review the "List of 100." What began with gasps of surprise as we read and discussed the five chosen as first tier turned into hoots and hollers as we realized the power of the intuitive methodology. We had selected people and companies that were at the very heart of research and product development in the area of sound, sight unseen. Our first tier list would help us validate our concepts, and permit us to move farther "outward" into the world of production. First things were first, arranged through intuitive selection.

- **Step 3: Develop the inspired information using both intuition and reason, as well as your other normal tools for understanding and analysis, returning to your gut feelings regularly to flesh out the original concept.**

As remarkable as our initial work turned out to be, we were now required to put a solid foundation under our inspired notions. This stage of the process often feels more tedious, because it does not always provide "Aha!" experiences every hour on the hour.

This is the phase of corroboration to determine the validity and reliability of those initial "hits." It is important to contact selected individuals deemed to be experts in the field, and to read massive amounts of material to determine if someone has already published or manufactured in the area in question.

We researched similar ideas, books, articles, and products. We contacted experts in the field who might be open to explore the concepts we were developing intuitively. We scoured the Internet, television, magazines, speeches, and news headlines for hints and clues to new technological developments that seemed related to what we were doing in our small corner of the world. We developed schematic representations from intuitive sessions and gradually turned those schematics into drawings that might make sense to a mainstream sound engineer. We hunted for discussions in mainstream science that might make our crazy ideas seem not so crazy at all.

Each time we would add a technical or potentially technical component from intuitive sources, we were required to track down any corroborative information from rational or technical sources as well. The intuitive information came so quickly and easily when compared to the more tedious tasks of grounding the work in the more acceptable worlds of science and technology. Those follow-up tasks were equally interesting and exciting, but certainly not quick.

Here is how Sylvia explains the process for her once the intuited portion is completed:

When I am transcribing [our sessions], I don't think about the content. However, when I read the printed copy, I get a better understanding of the language the group is going for. Paying attention to that is what's important to me. It is your [Helen's] translations that are the key to that flow.

For example, when the working permits me to adapt this thinking to images, like a 'kaleidoscope of fractals,' I put both kaleidoscope and fractal together in the Yahoo search box. That way of doing it links me to information more specific to what we're looking for, rather than just typing in one or the other alone. If the research results trigger several examples, I take it as being important. I have found that paying attention to that single/simple thing, links the research to where I will get the most beneficial results.

After that, I guess I would have to say that it's almost an automatic takeover that happens. I am moved along to other information, which could be thought of as just a lucky find, but I know it's all in the special attention from the get-go that moves me on to the rest, usually the best to be found.

I also ask Kevin after he has read the transcript what's most important for him to know more about, because his verbalizing usually includes a word or phrase that I wouldn't have thought of. For instance, he wanted to see a chart of elements. My pulling that up and just scanning it was a mini-lesson for me and opened up some new words (usually scientific language or just a code) that I'd jot down and add to the search.

I am never actually reading the site information, just scanning; my eyes always seem to focus on the information that I feel will be important. This happens with a one page or five page finding. Sometimes I will click off from a site and immediately pull it back up, give it another quick scan. More times than not, I print the information and realize it was a keeper, a source of good information.

Part of the site information will sometimes mention individuals or companies involved in whatever it's about. I jot them down and pull them up separately, which has sometimes given more insight into the timing of their findings or future interests, and tell us they may be possible future collaborators.

Something else that first surprised me was the timing of when I would find myself at the computer. I may have been moving towards a bike ride in the evening or relaxing with a book. I may have even been in the middle of something else when that feeling/little voice made its move, and all of a sudden I was at the computer and wouldn't rather be doing something else.

That's how it goes for me. The process for me is just staying open and available as it is with everything. The overall feel I get is just a hand-held thank you for paying attention. There is surely a helper with me.

Imagine Sylvia's talent for using words to describe an image that is only perceptible initially in the mind of the intuitive, who may have no professional experience in the specific field of inquiry, and no technical expertise to help translate the concept into meaningful terms for her! Then Sylvia (or a different colleague) works with the images and tracks down possible existing technologies or developments through Internet research, books, and articles. Clients may do the same following a session with me.

As for us, many hours of taped sessions, each refining the image or the concept further, went into the development of a single schematic for a "Souuund" product. Eventually there was sufficient information to complete a drawing that all colleagues could view and refine together. During the first phase, however, we would talk by telephone and record separately from two distant states, each deriving our own meaning from the words spoken, which would eventually add to our shared schematic image. One thing I know for sure: the time and money we spent was *nothing* compared to what would have been required to support a typical research and development lab!

It is astounding to discover how much "independent and interdependent invention" exists in the worlds of business and ideas. It is as if inventors, philosophers, and entrepreneurs are all watching the same conveyor belt of potentialities stream by their line of vision, ultimately selected or deselected for action on the basis of their particular desires, dreams, thoughts, beliefs, resources, and particular system of relevances about what is possible.

- **Return to framing intuitive questions based on the results of your searches and conversations concerning the next steps to take, individuals with whom to partner, anticipated strengths, weaknesses, opportunities, and threats to the success of the product.**

The process described above will go back and forth through many iterations among the team members as the concept or product takes form and becomes increasingly more sophisticated and real. There will be telephone and video calls, email correspondence, web searches, articles and books traded back and forth; and discussions with individuals who are not part of the team, but who suddenly "show up" with information that is relevant and exciting for the research and development team's purposes.

- **Use intuition as an aid for schematic drawings, materials development, modifications to scientific hypotheses based upon the new ideas, and other quite specific developments as well as more abstract purposes.**

> *[Excerpts from actual intuitive sessions about the UU device]*
> *H[elen]: Yes, the second product is the propulsion product that uses sound to generate energy. There is battery oriented electrical energy, solar, and wind energy, but no one has yet [2002] fully understood the power of sound energy as a propulsion device. The first is the palette product, to be used by composers and individuals who wish to create perfect sound around them. It also will be used with the much larger propulsion product. Both use the similar concept we've previously discussed regarding beehive*

technology. *The palette device produces an infinite number of sounds, which play upon the cells of human bodies, so that the ears, heart, mind, skin, bones and organs are all used in the production of sound. Some of these sounds are only heard in certain locations in the body, or through certain kinds of tissues or elements like the ear or eye structures. Bone marrow is a beehive concept within the core of the physical body. Bone marrow can make sound. The sound that creates the feeling of home is played at a cellular level through the existing structures of the body. Hair follicles hear, and the UUU palette is designed for total hearing.*

H: *Let's pick up thoughts from our last conversation that need to be cleared up now. What thoughts or images do you see relative to device # 1? What lingers in your mind and needs to be cleared up?*

K[evin]: *I feel very clear so far. We left off with the beehive. Would it be "mossy cadmium" we'd be using in the beehive?*

H: *There's another.*

K: *OK, I'm going to have to look them up. There's a sheet, a ball, and something else. I thought it might be what is called "mossy cadmium" because it is porous and used for electroplating."*

H: *It's used for electroplating? Excellent. The concept is correct, but it feels as if there's a patented next generation of this device or process. Find that.*

K: *OK, more towards the electroplating, rather than [whether] it's mossy?*

H: *Well, it's porous, but there is some electroplating that is made from metallic liquids that are not porous. With this kind, there is a process of etching that creates grooves into which information can be poured, if you want to use that analogy. There are receptors and holders, and in a sense micro caverns in which sound bounces off and out. So,*

> it's the combination of a product, superimposed on something that also, in its very nature, creates spaces, that forms this beehive concept. There will be a kind of electroplating upon the surface, so if you're looking on the top you'll see the openings. It is as if you paint the top surface of the beehive, but the chambers within are still there. Some of the interior walls will be painted by this blue cadmium element and some will not be painted. This variation will determine or affect sound quality.

K: OK, I understand. Tell me more about the little dots that stick up.

[Non-sequential excerpt from the beehive concept:]

H: Following the concept of the sponge, it's as if you have a plain sponge and you take a brush and you paint over it. The plain sponge has the dots as a part of the structure of the sponge itself. *[additional details deleted]* You take this painted material and put it into the beehive form.

These were very specific discussions about materials and structure. Some discussions, however, are much more abstract and far ranging. They eventually lead to specific design elements, but in the initial stages may seem to go quite far afield. You must also remember that we were discussing topics for which I had absolutely no scientific expertise, so we had to be patient with each other as we slogged through the theoretical issues that would ultimately become the foundation of the product under development.

What follows now is an excerpt from a subsequent session with Kevin and Sylvia, regarding the perhaps prevalent belief at the time that there is no sound in a vacuum. As you will notice on reading, the discussion here is much more abstract and not directly related to a specific design question for that day's meeting.

H: *The fundamental issue is one simple question: are vacuums empty? Our response to any who ask is, "Absolutely and resoundingly not."*

*Sound exists in vacuums, and units of potentiality exist in vacuums before they are pushed into matter. Vacuums hold pre-matter in the form of potentiality, intention, consciousness and thought. Once thought or intention leaves the vacuum, it joins the ranks of measurable units of matter, whether neutrinos or quarks or something yet to be discovered. Vacuums do hold energy. But the energy is not material energy, it is incipient potentially materialized energy. It is **potential** matter, **potential** transformed energy that at some moment becomes visible whether or not [the energy is] measurable in the three-dimensional world, or five-dimensional world, or twenty-dimensional world.*

K: *And that begins with intention?*

H: *Intention is the substance of the vacuum.*

K: *And that is followed by thought, words?*

H: *Intention is consciousness, intention is thought. Sound takes intention and propels it outward into material reality. It is sound that is capable of alchemy, that moves thought, conscious awareness, potentiality, probability into expression in the explicate order. Thought arises from and results in specific configurations of energy that must be ordered to have meaning. This movement of energy to frame one thought instead of another has sound, whether framed in words or abstractions, and it is the motion and propulsion of sound that makes the material possible.*

Vacuums are teeming with sound. Scientists are misguided and must give up the obsession with measurement in order to discover true properties of sound. This will come with great difficulty because measurement is a cornerstone of the rational mind. Without motion nothing leaves the vacuum, and nothing enters or leaves the black hole, which is the container of material worlds.

> *The vacuum is the container of non-material worlds.*
> *It is only precocious motion that is powerful enough to*
> *push a potentiality into material expression, and motion*
> *produces sound. Do you understand?*

In the foregoing you see examples of working in detail, through the intuitive process, to begin to flesh out concepts, products, and refinements regarding very specific ideas for the introduction of new products into the marketplace. The discussions are sometimes abstract, with no clear linkage to pragmatic outcomes, but rather offering perhaps some clue to further research in a field of inquiry. At other times they address materials, shape, color, and usage in quite specific terms. The range of intuitive guidance is quite broad: with practice, mastery, and fine-tuning, the potential contributions to business and science are immeasurable.

Go to the Future and See the Finished Product

- ○ What does it look like? _____
- ○ Who produced it? (names, initials, companies) _____
- ○ What was successful about the product? _____
- ○ Knowing then what you wish you knew now, what adjustments should you make in your design? _____

Financing and Marketing the Future Product

- ○ Where did you find venture capital? _____
- ○ How did you market the product? _____
- ○ What was the principal market segment for this product?

_____

Dreams and Business Intuition

I n using dreams for business applications of intuition, I find that a question or issue will "percolate" in my rational mind for a few days or even weeks, and then I will consciously decide to "sleep on it."

Being thoughtful to have writing paper and a good pen handy beside the bed in advance, I will take a nap or sleep through the night, and will just *know* when I wake up that a certain phrase or series of images is aimed at the client issue I had been mulling over. There is simply a different quality to the images or phrases, and I know this is meant not so much for me, but for my client.

Discernment is key. I remember one particularly powerful dream from which I woke up knowing that the dream was meant *both* for me personally, as well as for my client. When I sent the intuitive write-up later to the client I said, "This is what I got: I know some of this is meant for me, but I feel it is also relevant for you as well ... FWIW [for what it's worth]." I let the client know that there could be bias in the information because some of it seemed so relevant to me personally, which is not always the case; on the other hand, one of the earliest tenets of my intuition training was, "Don't edit." So I sent the unedited information, along with the disclaimer. The client later told me that what I sent him was also relevant, accurate, and as important for him to know as it was for me.

Given the nature of synchronicity and the fact that I seem to be *bombarded* with synchronous events in my daily life, it is also not uncommon for me to have a dream or conversation about a particular issue hours or days before an issue comes up in a session with a client for whom I have no advance information. Routinely I find that in some ways I had "met" that person in the dream state before our meeting over the phone, on Skype, or in person, and was getting prepared for our later real-time conversation through intuitive and precognitive dreams, as well as through apparently chance conversations, newspaper articles, or television snippets that I would just "stumble upon" in the waking state around that time, for no apparent reason.

Meet the Boss

Almost a year before I made a major move from the East Coast to California, I had a dream in which a figure appeared and asked me the question, "Shall we try it?" I jotted down in my dream journal a date that popped up in the dream: "September 18, 1981." At the time I was doing post-doctoral work at Harvard, with plans to look for permanent work once the year was over, but had no concrete plans to move to the West Coast. In fact, as I looked back today at my dream journals, I read that I was planning to work in New York City.

In September 1981 I began a new job at a university in the San Francisco Bay Area. About three years after the move I was rummaging through my dream journals, and there it was: the date September 18, 1981, as well as the question, "Shall we try it?" The person in the dream, who was a stranger to me at the time of the dream, was to become my new boss on that very date!

The Seven Second Strategic Plan

I cannot begin to calculate the endless hours spent in various versions of strategic planning over the decades of my full-time institutional work. If you own or work in a business or non-profit institution, I daresay you have a similar story.

Here is the moment when I ask you to try something different. Look at the following set of questions and write down the very first thought that pops into your head as you go through the list. Don't think, don't mull over your answers, just fill in the blanks quickly and without any hesitation.

"What is the strongest division or function of my company in rank order of strength, regardless of placement in the hierarchy?" You may scan an organization chart or directory to get you started. If you do look at the chart, scan quickly; don't analyze.

1. _____
2. _____
3. _____
4. _____
5. _____
6. _____
7. _____
8. _____
9. _____

Why is No. _____ strongest???

"What is the weakest division or function of my company in rank order?" You may use an organization chart or directory, but again, scan quickly. You might even just see where your eyes land and begin there.

1. _____
2. _____
3. _____
4. _____
5. _____
6. _____
7. _____
8. _____

Why is No. _____ weakest??

"What do I want to *start* doing, being, saying, producing?"

_____
_____
_____
_____
_____
_____

"What do I want to STOP doing, being, saying, producing?"

_____
_____
_____
_____
_____
_____

"What is my greatest fear about starting or stopping something?"

Starting_____

_____

_____

Stopping_____

_____

_____

_____

"What single action on my part, if any, would turn my company around?"

_____

_____

_____

_____

_____

_____

_____

"What single action on my part, if any, would turn my *life* around?"

_____

_____

_____

_____

_____

_____

_____

That, my friend, is the skeleton of a strategic plan. If you really did it right and wrote down the *very* first thoughts that popped into your mind as you answered these questions, you learned something about yourself and your business. This intuitive knowledge will shape your next moves, however simple or complex they might seem on the surface, regardless of the size of your company, your family, or your wallet.

What If My Intuition Doesn't Work?

Sometimes—rarely—intuitive guidance doesn't work for you as well as usual, or as well as you would like. Perhaps you yourself are not focused sufficiently (did you remember to take that breath?); or perhaps the buddy you ask for help can't help; or perhaps that client just doesn't want to hear what you have to offer; or perhaps it's just a bad fit. How much is right? How much is wrong? What to do?

Notice quickly, take a break for a while, and try again.

Or . . . move on. If you feel stuck, just let the whole thing go and wait until a moment when you feel unstuck or you feel like you do have a good fit. If possible, forget about it completely for now and go back at a later time. Sometimes "later" could be as brief as ten minutes later; at other times you may need days to completely clear your head and your expectations.

Not too long ago I did a session with a client when things simply didn't work: the electronics didn't work; the information didn't work for the client or me; and it became clear fairly early on that this simply was not a good fit. This has happened for me perhaps five or six times in the past 30 years. The feeling is unmistakable. The key here: *just let it go.*

- If you have asked a buddy whose response simply makes no sense
- If you feel a client is simply closed to the information you have to offer.
- If you are just plain WRONG . . .

Let it go and move on. Pay attention to the signals that something isn't working and continue to develop your discernment skills. You can try it later with the same person successfully—that has happened for me several times. Or you can say, "This just won't work" and move on.

Just as businesses and people have a natural life cycle, intuition has its own rhythms as well. Holding on for dear life intuitively makes no sense when it has become clear that holding on right now serves no purpose. Let go without judgment or blame and move on. Sometimes you are not meant to work together: you may speak a different language of the soul, or come from a different emotional "planet." Eventually everything gets sorted out.

If you are one of those individuals who is being paid for intuitive information and not just playing intuitive games with a friend, then do not charge your clients when this happens, or return their money if they have prepaid. You might also offer the client another complimentary session a few months later to see if something has changed between you. That is, of course, only if they and you are interested in another try.

By the way, just because things don't work, it does not necessarily mean that the intuitive information was wrong. It could be that the *timing* simply was not right for the information to be received, and the client needed time to mull over what he or she was told.

On one occasion a client came to me who was so angry following our session that he threw the tape into the garbage can outside our meeting place. A few months later, however, he was back, laughingly told my host the story about the garbage can, and we have worked together very successfully ever since.

Things did not work out so well with another client. I just know we were not and perhaps will never be a match, for any variety of possible reasons. Unlike the earlier case, I do not expect this person to come back, and have moved on to the next intuitive challenge. Sometimes that's just the way it is. Sometimes the client is entrenched in testing mode, expecting, allowing and receiving nothing. There will always be other moments to tickle your fancy and remind you how good and intuitive you are, so . . .

Tuck your ego in your pocket. Learn from the experience, whether positive or negative or somewhere in between, and KEEP MOVING. Don't over-analyze, don't get scared, and especially don't get stuck in the fear that somehow you are no good, or you are not intuitive. If you are breathing, intuition is your birthright, so keep at it. Many wonderful opportunities for fun and mastery lie ahead!

Epilogue: Integrity and Seven Second Decision Making

In many ways, integrity is the most important component of all when considering the use of intuitive decision making for business and personal success. In keeping to integrity, we can use intuitive abilities to exercise trust, discernment, and timing in order to navigate our way.

Trust, discernment, and timing rest on a foundation of good intention. You may find yourself asking the question, "How can I trust my gut feeling, and my own integrity, when I understand so little about the intuitive process and doubt my ability to use it properly?" The very fact that you frame such a question in the first place is a good indication that you are already acting with integrity, and that your actions are grounded in good intention. You care about your ability to serve properly, and you care about the impact of any decision you make on the well being of the company. This is a perfect place to start.

Trust

Look around you and see if there are individuals working with and for you who match your integrity, individuals you trust to help you on this journey to opening up your mind to new possibilities. Initially you may only be able to think of one person you would risk confiding in about such possibilities, whether or not you and that person work in the same company. However, if you typically make good business decisions, if you share and delegate responsibility appropriately, realizing that you are not "the only one," if you have acted on a hunch before and that hunch was on the mark, then you know what success feels like and are well on your way to adding the regular and accurate use of intuition to your business life. And now you will have good company to help you with this.

If you have not experienced any or all of these successes, start now to trust yourself and others. Use the tips and techniques in this book a bit at a time to build that infrastructure in a regular business context. Remember, many of these tools are just good business practice with a twist. Then branch out to find somebody who can play with you as you develop this new intuitive tool. Start with smaller decisions and see how they work first, and then expand to broader and more consequential ones. Start with issues and people you already feel pretty comfortable about, and then stretch to situations in which you feel a bit less confident. Use double-blind intuitive tools first and as much as possible until you learn to trust yourself more. Make a game of it, and keep things light.

You might start with games that are not directly associated with work, such as paying attention to strangers at a restaurant or at the airport, and making up stories about them. What are they like? What issues are they facing? How do they appear to feel? There is nothing to corroborate here, just an opportunity to let your mind fly and start blathering. I do not expect you to approach these people to find out if you were right! Remember, you are just opening a new neural pathway.

You don't have to play intuitive games with your entire staff all at once, or even mention directly what you are up to. Start with a friend at work, or who might even be with a different company, but who might be open to trade off with you and be in on the use of your intuitive tools.

Assume your own good intention throughout, and you will find it reflected back to you in your daily encounters. Like all of us, you will make some mistakes, but that is normal. Intuition does not eliminate mistakes, but it certainly helps avoid some humdingers.

As you begin slowly and thoughtfully and playfully, your trust of yourself and of others will deepen. Keep track of hits and misses, and notice any patterns that emerge. For example, you might get the content right but miss the timing, or get the timing right but miss the surprise factor that fueled the situation. Everybody does better at some things than others, so pay attention to what you do best and build on those skills. Your intuition "score" will probably be higher in content areas about which you feel most knowledgeable technically and, surprisingly, in areas that are just too far fetched to be anything *except* intuition. The middle ground is the murkiest. That is why I often say, "The less I know the better." The result *must* be the result of intuitive information, because I could not otherwise be accurate in such a far-flung domain.

The more you play well and successfully, the more you will come to trust yourself and your hunches. It is as simple as that. When you have good intention as your foundation, you will do little damage beyond the range of chance in the worst case, and you will certainly speed up your learning curve for utilizing intuition effectively in the best-case scenario.

Discernment

By no means do I wish to underestimate the importance of discernment in all of this. You must come to know yourself and your deeply held beliefs and interests in order to use intuition properly. Cultural background, religion, peer pressure, and the conventional business environment are important in shaping these beliefs and interests. It is critical that you learn to discern "what's mine and what's yours" as you sift through probabilities and interpretations of intuitive information. For example, if you think someone is about to leave a position and you want that job, then you must factor in your self-interest in taking an intuitive look at who the successor is likely to be. This would be a perfect time to use a double-blind technique and the help of a friend to sort things out.

How do you tell if some probability or potential acquisition is really feasible? You have to trust—really trust—the first answer you get and go with it. This trust will happen over time through trial and error, and the errors will diminish. Remember the earlier story about the commodities trader who insisted that the price of oil could not reach the intuitive number I gave him in a year? While the number was unlikely, it was certainly possible: it happened. The key in that situation was whether the individual trusted himself and his investment strategy, whether he trusted my intuitive advice or not, whether he trusted me personally, and whether I trusted myself in giving him such a farfetched answer. Luckily for me, I knew nothing about the domain, so there were no "facts" to cloud my judgment. On the other hand, there were hits as well as misses with this or any other client, so discernment about my own strengths and weaknesses is important as well. For example, I noticed that I was more accurate with long-term than short-term rates and prices. I routinely perform better on intermediate and longer-term tasks than near-term, and love reading the news to find that a prediction given years earlier was happening as I had seen, and often within the timeframe predicted.

Timing

Which brings us back to the issue of timing, the third of the key elements in using intuition with integrity: trust, discernment, and timing.

You may have the right information, and you may be able to discern with confidence that a particular plan of action is right for your company. That plan might fail, however, if you don't get the timing right. I have already mentioned how tricky timing can be in sorting out intuitive and non-intuitive information. That is why trusting *yourself* is key. It is the first among elements to sort out and get clear about as you consider issues of potential conflicts of interest and timing. With all the other factors at play, the last thing you need is a lack of confidence in your own integrity. Let your intuition help you with issues of timing, and these tools are powerful indeed, but they only work if you permit them to function unencumbered by self-doubt.

I am reminded of the old Shakespeare quotation from *Macbeth*, "If chance will have me king, why, chance may crown me without my stir."[18] On the one hand, Macbeth counted on chance or fate to get him where he really wanted to be. Then he proceeded to kill off anyone and anything that got in his way. That was not the exercise of chance, nor was it the exercise of integrity. The appropriate use of intuition crowns you without your having to pay some heavy-duty consequences down the road. It does this through the proper use of trust, discernment, and timing, all resting on a foundation that assumes and expects integrity.

I have learned the hard way—first hand—that integrity is key, or the regret from falling out of integrity can last for decades. I have also learned that these personal, unintended, and usually unconscious lapses helped me clarify my own principles and boundaries, even at the temporary expense of others. Where possible, I have asked forgiveness and made amends; where this has not been possible, I have attempted to "pay it forward." I have also permitted myself to forgive others who have been unethical with me, even if continuing "self-righteous anger" would be considered acceptable and understandable. There are always ongoing opportunities to learn and to refine integrity in belief and action. So do not be too hard on yourself while you work with training wheels still attached to your bicycle!

How can you trust, and how can you be trustworthy, knowing your *own* weaknesses and failures, let alone the less than stellar behavior of others that you witness daily? Accomplish this by adopting a threshold stance that expects and recognizes the fundamental good intention in your own behavior and the behavior of others, supported by the consistent practice of discernment and the consistent goal of total integrity, even if it remains unattainable. Expect the best, but do not deny it when less than the best presents itself to you or to your customers and friends. Through the use of intuition, draw out the best potentialities for all concerned.

Individuals in all domains trample ethical boundaries routinely, and some are apparently never brought to task for these breaches of conduct. Do not worry about them and what does or does not happen to them. Just focus on your own interior flame and let the rest go: what goes around eventually comes around in one form or another, and you have neither time nor interest in rubbernecking somebody else's consequences. Besides, like you, they may come to understand better down the road. As Oprah Winfrey like to say as she quotes Maya Angelou, "When you know better, you do better." I have learned to do better, and so can you. So give yourself a break and keep going!

The use of intuition does raise other ethical questions, however:

- Is intuition an invasion of privacy?
- If everybody can and does use his or her intuitive capacity, will society deteriorate in a futuristic nightmare scenario, where intuition is simply the latest military weapon?
- Can intuition really become a tool for discernment and for identifying the basic good intention present in all of humanity?
- Is it possible to be fully expressed without oppressing others?

It is my opinion and deeply held belief that intuition is not an invasion of privacy for several reasons:

- Nothing, including intuition, takes away the right and authority of the individual to know and to be known. My professional colleagues all agree that it is impossible to "read" someone who does not wish to be read, or to know someone who chooses not to be known.

- On the other hand, it is also my belief that most individuals deeply *wish* to be known and understood, whether in the workplace or at home. It is this deeper wish that permits us to retrieve intuitive information that ultimately benefits both individual and company. Again, the assumption of good intent is key, and well as the ability to discern presenting issues from deeper expressions of desire. When your "whole life is a prayer," as I stated in Part One of this book, then looking at the private yearnings and fears of individuals in your life and in the world ultimately supports your mutual success. This is entirely different from "prurient interest."

- When a client comes to me and asks something about himself, or about "Mary" in some distant location, I do not feel I am invading either his space or Mary's, any more than I feel I am invading the space of a potential company that is looking to partner with a business client. The goal is the best outcome for all parties, and in that space outside of space and time and normal reason, I am able to see factors and solutions that would otherwise go unnoticed. The same is true for you.

- Likewise, when agencies of government conduct remote viewing experiments on another, there must be some shared belief in their country's service to the world *on the part of both parties*, which makes these sites or weapons locatable to the remote viewer. I cannot fully explain it yet, but there is a kind of interior and transnational system of checks and balances, even if totally subconscious, that ultimately keeps us from blowing each other and ourselves up when we have an opportunity to do so.

- In my worldview, clients and subjects give permission in advance, often in the dream state, or in the latent world of possibilities; otherwise we would not be meeting at all. If they truly did not want me to help them understand an issue or solve a problem, we would, in a manner of speaking, be "invisible" to each other for the purposes of a consultation.

I will reserve a deeper explanation of this worldview for another time, and perhaps another book. For the time being, however, suffice it to say that this is the understanding within which I operate, and which I believe makes it possible to use the universal capacity for intuition with integrity.

The tool of intuition is a neutral one; the responsibility for its use is up to us. It is my core belief that all individuals, families, nations, and companies want neither more nor less than to be fully expressed; or as Abraham Maslow would say, to be "self-actualized."[19]

When intuition is used properly, it assists in the process of self-actualization at every level, especially when intuition is partnered with discernment, a belief in the good intention of others, trust in one's own worthiness, and a core belief in infinite possibilities for personal and professional success.

I believe that each of us gets to experience a personal world according to an individualized and fundamental worldview. I must use the word "believe" here, because I am not a physicist capable of proving these things. It is this core belief that supports my corollary belief that it is possible to be fully expressed without oppressing others. There is *literally* enough to go around—or not—depending on my individualized worldview. I may choose to live in a world of scarcity because I want to make a difference and end it; or because I want to invent a new product that will make me a lot of money and at the same time fill some human need. Or I may choose to live in a world of abundance by having a lot of money and institutional resources even if others are suffering from poverty. Or I could choose to live simply and need relatively little. Or I could arrive at some experience in between.

If I assume human nature to be depraved, then human beings will show me that aspect or variation of themselves. On the other hand, if I believe human nature to be cooperative and based on good intent, then that is the world I will come to experience as well. These are essentially the same human beings, but expressed differently through my perception, depending on my particular worldview. People trapped in the Convention Center in New Orleans during hurricane Katrina experienced a literal "hell on earth" when fear took over and the very worst of human nature was called out. When miners were trapped underground in Peru for a very long time, what might have turned into a dog-eat-dog struggle became instead an opportunity for cooperation and innovation. In both cases the world was watching, and in both cases definitions and expectations of the deepest elements of human nature offered us all a look at ourselves.

In literally seven seconds or less, the answers to some of these otherwise impenetrable and timeless questions can begin to unravel, offering solutions that the rational mind alone simply could not fathom. The explanation for this limitation on the part of reason stems from the fact that there is so much more to the human mind, as well as brain, than some of us have ever imagined. (I think it is safe to use the word "fact" here.) We cannot create solutions to the Whole, using only five or ten per cent of the tools in our experience-making toolkit. Ethical solutions require the expansion of our understanding and of our capacities for knowing, whether or not we know exactly how we know.

Accessing information in seven seconds or less bypasses the locks and limitations of reason, and it makes another exciting tool for discovery available. Science and metaphysics are beginning to offer hints at such possibilities with trending notions of probable and parallel universes, multiverses, the possibility that we have counterpart, probable, and reincarnational selves, time travel, and other completely *outrageous* approaches to understanding our world and to solving our seemingly intractable problems.

We could continue along what seems to be our current path, exhausting the resources on earth and attempting to colonize other planets in the same way we have colonized this one. We could do that and be scientifically thrilled and justified in our behavior from a particular point of view.

Alternatively, we could skip into that infinite space of the unfettered mind and find solutions that do not require colonization, genocide, the destruction of intellectual and cultural history, and the starvation of others to feel safe in our world. Perhaps that probable world already exists and we could simply travel there with or without spaceships and ask them how they did it. We could meet future versions of our companies and products and policies and find out ahead of time how they worked out—or not. We could begin to create future success and abundance in this moment teeming with possibility.

Then, using the information from our flights into fancy, we could make certain adjustments *now* to our process, product line, social policy, energy consumption, and framework of knowledge that would end up shifting the very foundation of our definition of human nature, animal existence, and the qualities of organic and inorganic matter, as well as the qualities of energy and consciousness. The universe would open itself up to us in such new ways that we would have *plenty* to explore instead of slashing and burning our people, animals, and natural resources, all as a result of distorted good intention.

New categories of business could spring up to replace old ones whose natural life cycle had ended. We might actually become the limitless consciousness we already are, the new human we have actually always been.

In my world, fear of lack is obsolete because, like the elements in a Jungian dream, all of the characters in my environment, whether ten yards or ten thousand miles away, represent some aspect of me. I can only be truly fulfilled when the Whole, when every character and element in my dream, feels fulfilled as well. In my world, that future already exists, and I intend to go there and see it expressed. Intuition is the small gift in my hand to help me get there.

So for me, learning to decipher and use intuitive information in seven seconds or less to enhance business, frontier science, and quality of life is a thrilling enterprise! Perhaps this individual action on my part will trigger a thousand more probable worlds in which there is more than enough to go around, remembering as its fundamental motto: "Experience is based on collaborative good intention."

Acknowledgments

Without the support of the following people, this book would not be. It is as simple as that. Sunyeen Pai, who has become sun, moon, devil's advocate, digital librarian and researcher extraordinaire, teacher, supporter, paradise builder, dearest friend; "Henry," who even now cannot be named for all the reasons that are the subject of the book: mainstay, loyal supporter, true friend, trustworthy ally, best client imaginable; Laura Messina and Teresa Puentes, whose love and friendship literally kicked me out of a musty closet and jump started a whole new phase of life for me; the Zurich Group, especially Corinne Frey and Rachna in 't Veld (the rest of you know who you are!) for breakthrough after breakthrough, and for opportunities to share what I have learned. The tranquil lives of Kip Eddy and Sue Phillips were thrown completely upside down when they began supporting and working with me. There are no words to express my deepest gratitude and heartfelt sadness that Kip did not live to see his dreams fulfilled, and that Sue had to see so many of hers demolished.

How lucky I am to have been welcomed into new circles of friends here in Hawaii! Smart, funny, talented folks are teaching me to enjoy the land, music, good weather, good company, and good food. Sadly, it is unlikely any of them will succeed in teaching me to play the ukulele well, but what fun to try! The folks at Coffee Talk on a little corner in Kaimuki Town here in Honolulu had no clue what I was doing there every day, drinking endless cups of coffee with an occasional gingerbread muffin. Thanks to them for their pet-friendly, writing friendly, unhurried, welcoming environment.

In her own inimitable style, Charlene Cain offered me the freedom to live and love and write again. I believe she literally sacrificed a potentially longer life so I could do this. And so did Chaco, the four-legged wonder. I am riding on the wings and shoulders of countless clients, colleagues, and friends who taught and helped me to be fully expressed at last.

Thanks to my European hosts for putting up with the endless traffic through their spaces and hearts, especially Françoise Heyberger, Jean Guil, Andy Maleta, Christl Lieben, Corinne Frey, Silvia Scheid, Miren Lavaud, David and Marie Delbaere, Didier and Rosemarie Banos, Khadijah and Rudra, and Marie-Christine Ginibre. My Aruban hosts also were amazing, introducing me to a country that I have come to love deeply. Juliet Chieuw and Jose began the journey; Richard and Lin Visser, Louella Brezovar, Peter and Marjam Auwerda, Adi Rasmijn, and Ingrid Werleman continued and supported my work there. While much of my work in the U.S.A. took place locally where I lived, others hosted me in other locations throughout the country: Rosemary Slabaugh and Mary Gray, Helen Davis, Lynne Moon, Eddie Penn, and Marlin McKenna and Doug Lonngren. So many good people and amazing experiences have come into my life through the generosity of my hosts in the U.S. and abroad!

There are others who helped shape my intellectual and metaphysical history. Some are no longer alive except through my fond memories of them: C. Pamela Crandall, Egon Bittner, Elizabetha "Lisa" Werner, Jane Roberts, Robert F. Butts, and Wale Taiwo. My parents, James E.W. and Juanita Hampton Stewart, taught me in depth about Christianity and the power of asking questions. They also provided the opportunity for me to explore from a very young age so many corners of the world and its varied approaches to knowledge and spirituality. Although they are no longer physically present, my parents' sacrifice and unwavering adherence to principle are a constant reminder to me as I work in the world. Perhaps I can help ease the burden of impossible and painful either-or choices by introducing into ordinary life the possibility of a principled "both-and" worldview.

Dearest mentors and friends Tamara Diaghilev, Mietek Wirkus, Sanaya Roman, Duane Packer, Don Wismer, Mike Brown, Tim Fish, Mary Dillman, Lee Bolman, Les Samuel, and Rebecca Knuth are still very much alive, and may not even be aware how much they have influenced my work. Nancy Ashley nudged me to focus and to get to a single voice for this creative endeavor, instead of my usual seventeen. She and several others read and commented on this manuscript in very helpful ways: Sunyeen Pai, Laura Messina, Don Wismer, Lynne Hara Moon, Bill Gregoricus, Anet Dunne, Carolyn Tett, Jeffrey Frick, Sally Rundle, and Arden Reece.

I owe a special debt of gratitude to those members of my family of origin who could have dismissed me as simply crazy, but who decided to hang in there even when it was unclear who I was exactly, and where I might be going with all this intuition "stuff." After all, my parents invested so much preparing me to become a respected educator, not a misunderstood intuitive. My uncle Lawrence Hampton is my anchor when it comes to matters of family and heart. My aunts Sally Hampton Brooks, Helen Bowen Hampton, and Antoinette Allen Hampton mean the world to me, as does my heart sister Christine Harris.

Sadé Cain is not crazy like me; she is *horse* crazy! Sadé is an equestrian eventer, teacher, and storyteller in her own right. Her exemplary qualities as a young human being—wise, compassionate, persevering—remind and assure me the future will be in good hands. How proud I am to call her daughter and granddaughter, even though I did not bring her into the world. She could have held me back; but she offered butterflies instead.

Last, but certainly not least, the staff at Balboa Press have been responsive and supportive far beyond what authors typically come to expect from publishing houses. Heather Perry walks on water as far as I am concerned. She is a consummate professional who moved the process along skillfully, quickly, and comfortably.

Resources

- Books - Recommended
  - Blanchard, Kenneth and Johnson, Spencer, 1982, *The One Minute Manager*. NY: William Morrow and Company
  - Bolman, Lee G., and Deal, Terrence E., August, 2011. *Leading with Soul: an Uncommon Journey of Spirit, 3rd edition.* San Francisco: Jossey-Bass/Wiley.
  - Bolman, Lee G., and Gallos, Joan V., 2011, *Reframing Academic Leadership.* San Francisco: Jossey-Bass/Wiley.
  - Bolman, Lee G., and Deal, Terrence E., 2012, *Reframing Organizations: Artistry, Choice and Leadership.* San Francisco: Jossey-Bass/Wiley
  - Christensen, Clayton M., 1997, *The Innovator's Dilemma.* New York: Harper Business.
  - Christensen, Clayton M., Scott D. Anthony, and Erik A. Roth, 2004, *Seeing What's Next.* Boston, MA: Harvard Business School Press.
  - Damian-Knight, Guy, 1986, *The I Ching on Business and Decision Making.* Rochester, Vermont: Destiny Books.
  - Dator, James A., Ed., 2002, *Advancing Futures: Futures Studies in Higher Education*, Westport CT: Praeger.
  - Day, Laura, 1996, *Practical Intuition: How to Harness the Power of Your Instinct and Make it Work for You.* New York: Broadway Books.
  - Friedman, Norman, 1997, *Bridging Science and Spirit: Common Elements in David Bohm's Physics, The Perennial Philosophy and Seth.* Oregon: The Woodbridge Group.

- Gladwell, Malcolm, 2005, *Blink: The Power of Thinking Without Thinking*. New York: Little, Brown.
- Heider, John, 1986. *The Tao of Leadership: Leadership Strategies for a New Age.*
- Kaku, Michio, 2009, *Physics of the Impossible*. New York: Anchor Books.
- Kaku, Michio, 2012, *Physics of the Future*. New York: Anchor Books.
- Frantz, Roger, and Pattakos, Alex, eds., 1998, *Intuition at Work: Pathways to Unlimited Possibilities.*
- Penney Peirce, 1997, *The Intuitive Way*. Hillsboro, Oregon: Beyond Words Publishing.
- Radin, Dean, 2006, *Entangled Minds: Extrasensory Experiences in a Quantum Reality*. New York: Paraview Pocket Books.
- Roberts, Jane, 1977, 1979, *The 'Unknown' Reality*, Vols. 1&2. Englewood Cliffs, NJ: Prentice-Hall.
- Schutz, Alfred, 1971, *Collected Papers: The Problem of Social Reality, Vol. 1*. The Hague: Martinus Nijhoff.
- Taleb, Nassim Nicholas, 2010, *The Black Swan: The Impact of the Highly Improbable,* New York: Random House Trade Paperbacks.
- Vaughan, Frances E., 1979, *Awakening Intuition*, NY: Anchor Books, Doubleday.

Endnotes

1. Gladwell, Malcolm, Blink: *The power of Thinking Without Thinking*, 2005.
2. Gladwell, pp. 189-244.
3. Radin, Dean, *Entangled Minds*, 2006, pp 142-145; 240-274.
4. Schutz, Alfred, *Collected Papers, Vol. 1*, 1971, p. 316.
5. Stewart, Helen L., *Buffering: The Leadership Style of Huey P. Newton, Co-Founder of the Black Panther Party*, University Microfilms International, 1980, p. 133
6. Wikipedia, http://en.wikipedia.org/wiki/Remote_viewing
7. Radin, Dean, *Entangled Minds*, 2006.
8. Bittner, Egon, *Police on Skid Row: A Study of Peace Keeping*. NJ Irvington Publishers, 1993, p. 29.
9. Dossey, Larry, *Healing Words*, 1994.
10. Day, Laura, *Practical Intuition*, 1996.
11. Humphrey, Albert, "SWOT Analysis for Management Consulting", *SRI alumni Newsletter*, (SRI International), 2005.
12. Blanchard, Kenneth and Johnson, Spencer, *The One Minute Manager*, 1982.
13. Roberts, Jane, *Unknown Reality, Vol 1*, p. 56
14. Taleb, Nassim Nicholas, *The Black Swan*, 2010.
15. Dator, James A., *Advancing Futures*, 2002, pp. 1-14,
16. Roberts, Jane, *Unknown Reality, Vol 1*, pp. 53-60.
17. "The Art of the Brilliant Hunch," *Business 2.0*, 2002.
18. *Macbeth*, Act I, Scene 3.
19. Maslow, Abraham H., 1968, *Toward a Psychology of Being*. NY: John Wiley & Sons.

Made in the USA
Las Vegas, NV
17 December 2023

83006501R00094